OVERCOME ANXIETY

This Book Includes:

The Essential Collection of Books to Stop Negative Thinking: Master Your Emotions, Master Your Thinking

By Jon Power

MASTER YOUR EMOTIONS

The Essential Guide on Self Help and Dark Psychology to Overcome Negativity and Anxiety. Improve Your Social Skills with Persuasion Techniques and Stop Procrastinating

By Jon Power

Summary

INTRODUCTION

If you are reading this right now, it means you're one of the people working too hard to get rid of frustration, pain, and insecurity and build a life of self-positivity. Okay, count on yourself fortunate because you've just reached your one-stop shop for everything you need to learn about handling frustration, fatigue, and anxiety; now you can find out all you need to know about overcoming depression. The book provides genuine information, ideas, tactics, and techniques that can help you create the healthy, negative-devoid, and deserving quality of life that you crave. The book is written in a concise and easy-to-digest language to help you easily assimilate all the contents inside.

The book will teach you everything you need to know about stress management, anxiety management, and anger management by making you privy to some of the most effective techniques and strategies for emotional intelligence mastery and learning. The book will start by explaining all the details that you need to learn about emotions; the essence of emotions; and the emotional origins. What's affecting our emotions? How do emotions evolve? Are negative emotions even needed? How do you get rid of these? You will find valid answers to these and many more questions in "Master your emotions: improve your emotional intelligence by controlling your mind and boosting your brain to eliminate your anxiety and worry."

We'll also take a close look at what emotional intelligence is, and how it can help you get rid of negativity in your life. Most importantly, to get rid of worries, concerns and uncertainties you'll learn about anger management and core relaxation strategies. We will give you tips on how to do awareness meditation, which is a common form of meditation now used for self-awareness practice, in order to further help. Mindfulness meditation technique can help you develop a connection with your inner self so you can develop a high intelligence of the emotions.

If you're interested in leading a valuable, qualitative and positive life; if you're interested in learning to project positivity into negative emotions and you'd like to learn how to be more productive, purposeful and positive in life but you don't know where to start from, this one-stop-shop for positivity promises to teach you these and all you need to know. In this incredible reading, any response you need is awaiting you.

Now it's up to you to choose a life without stress, anger, anxiety; a life of positivity; and start living with a de-cluttered and free mind using the strategies, tips, and techniques in the book that await you. Add a copy to the cart and set off on the road towards prosperity and positivity.

It wasn't until 1995, though, that emotional intelligence rolled into the mainstream consciousness and became a ground-breaking concept when Daniel Goleman published his book by the same name. At that time, the intelligence quotient was seen as the only factor that mattered when evaluating the capabilities of an individual. Once emotional intelligence had taken over, IQ was perceived as a narrow or limited way to assess the chances of success for an individual. The cut-throat career, job, and business world was very different from a classroom's cushy confines.

When one had to handle the real world they would have to adapt to a different kind of intelligence than the theoretical intelligence used in schools or libraries. The intelligence and cognitive abilities of one person alone did not guarantee success in life. A degree did not automatically mean a high paid job or a profitable enterprise.

At best, you are going to get your foot through the door. You'd need much more than plain intelligence, though, for someone to succeed. Raising the bar will include psychological, listening, interaction, and interpersonal skills. These are life skills that don't come in the classroom but are learned from staying in a hostel, sitting in pubs, attending social clubs, being a part of sports teams and volunteering.

Do you still believe that IQ is the only factor which determines the overall success of an individual in life? If that was true, every successful person you spot today should be a Harvard, Stanford, MIT graduate with a Ph.D. from the CEO of big organizations to the president, to thought leaders and successful entrepreneurs.

Make a list of 10 people you most admire. They are the people you look up to as they lead a life of success and balance. Are all of these folks graduates of distinguished educational institutions with a high IQ top honors? My money's on No! Do not get me wrong here, again. I don't undermine the importance of intelligence or ask you to close this mechanical engineering book and start reading about human psychology. When you actually possess high cognitive abilities and a high intelligence quotient, it's fantastic. All I'm thinking that, hopefully, you should have both EQ and IQ complementing each other to increase your chances of real-world achievement. If you can increase your emotional quotient to back up an intelligence quotient that is already strong, you will do many great things!

If you ask me to choose between two talents, however, I'd have to go with emotional intelligence. Within today's world, a person with average intelligence and highly evolved emotional intelligence has a better chance of succeeding than an individual with high intelligence and less developed emotional intelligence. Today's game name is about managing people, knowing their desires or motivations, and manipulating their thoughts to get the most positive outcomes.

Technical knowledge can help you direct and/or instruct your team to complete a task. The ability to keep them engaged by knowing their feelings will however ensure that they will remain empowered and successful throughout the cycle.

The cognitive intelligence or intellectual potential of a person has always been measured as being capable of retaining facts or making calculations. However, in certain positions, such as leadership and entrepreneurship, those skills are not necessarily all-encompassing. Tons of CEOs, world leaders and founders of Fortune 500 firms are dropouts from high school. If intellect alone were the measure of success for an individual, how would you justify that?

The reality is that it's not as straightforward as a single factor that determines our success, like intelligence. In fact, it is a combination of factors that are essentially emotional and social life skills that will help you to survive or thrive in the real world. Intelligence quotient is an inborn but not all-inclusive element which can affect the success in life of an individual.

This is good news, because regardless of your traditional, genetically determined intelligence, if you work on other social-emotional life skills, you have a good chance of being successful.

A high emotional quotient and other collections of social and psychological abilities will definitely boost your chances.

CHAPTER 1

WHAT ARE EMOTIONS?

Understanding the nature of the emotions and what emotions are is the first step towards learning how to master your emotions successfully. How could you learn something after all if you don't even know what it is, or how it works? In a simplified term, the Oxford dictionary states emotion is "a strong feeling deriving from one's situation, attitude, or interactions with others." You can already see from both meanings that emotions are in some way related to thoughts. Emotions and feelings aren't exactly the same though. Human emotions are usually triggered by changes in the physiological and behavioral structure of an individual.

Usually we as humans can tell our emotional state at any point. You know whether you feel happy, depressed or angry. What you may not be able to tell, though, is where exactly those feelings originate. Normally most of us make the mistake of doing the same thing to emotions and feelings. They even use both in the context of synonyms, interchangeably. However, as we said; emotions and feelings are two different things which depend somewhat on one another. Although feelings arise from a state of sub-consciousness and psychology, emotions are mostly intrinsic to perceptions and derive from a conscious state. Emotions can be called passive corporal responses to internal or external stimuli. So we can conclude that without feelings there may be emotions but without emotions there can be no feelings. Feelings are subjects of the state of our emotions.

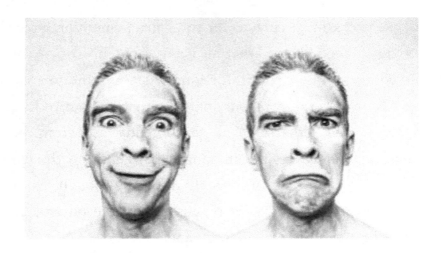

THE FOUR KEY EMOTIONS

Each human experience of emotion has four important components that are: cognitive, behavioral, physiological, and affect reactions. Normally, when you feel an emotion it is caused and fueled by any of these four elements.

Firstly, emotional cognitive reaction refers to the way a person thinks, stores information and experiences, and perceives an event. Behavioral responses refer to how people express an emotion in the first place. On the other hand, physiological reactions are triggered by changes in a person's hormonal level. Finally, affecting reactions signifies the emotional state and the very nature of the emotion. That part of the emotions normally activates the other as described. Let's say, for example, that an aunt you don't like comes to visit your parents; you see that person immediately, you automatically think in your mind that she's annoying or scary, probably because of past experiences with her and her disposition (this is a cognitive reaction). Because of that perception of your annoying aunt, you become grumpy (this is the reaction to the effect). Your parents then come to tell you that your aunt should stay in the house for a while; you feel your blood rising in indignation (this is a physiological reaction) and you leave quickly for your room (behavioral reaction). To understand the various components of the emotions, you must make sure that you know where emotions originate. Researchers have tried using different theories to identify the source of the feelings. Such theories try to explain the mechanisms of formulating feelings, the emotional origins and the cause. Though not in-depth, we will be digging into these hypotheses. We'll attempt to understand how isolated feelings exist.

Scientists have proposed various theories in the bid to understand feelings, which are categorized in three main categories. We have the physiological theories that suggest that emotions are the result of certain responses within the body; there are the neurological theories that suggest that certain activities taking place in the brain are responsible for our emotions; finally, there are theories under the cognitive class that believe that our thoughts, perceptions and mental activities are responsible for the emotions

The first hypothesis that attempts to explain feelings is the' evolutionary theory of feeling' developed by a naturalist, Charles Darwin. This hypothesis suggests that emotions develop because of their biological function that encourages human reproduction and longevity. Darwin also said that humans seek to reproduce with mates because of the feelings of love and affection that are emotional products. He also clarified that feelings of fear are forcing people to recognize danger and run. We have emotions according to Darwin, because we need them to adapt and survive in whatever environment we are in. Emotions trigger appropriate responses to certain environmental stimuli, thereby fostering our chances of survival. We have to be mindful of our own feelings and those of others to live in any environment. Nevertheless, being conscious of emotions isn't enough, we also need to be able to properly perceive, monitor, and respond to a stimulus. Being able to interpret our emotions correctly and that of others allows us to give appropriate and appropriate responses to any situation we find ourselves in.

Next is the principle of James-Lange which is a popular hypothesis in emotional physiology. This theory was put forward individually by physiologist Carl Lange and psychologist William James. The James-Lange emotion theory argues that emotions are bodily responses that are triggered by the physiological reactions of the body to certain events. The emotions you produce in response to a physiological reaction caused by a stimulus in the environment depend on your physiological reaction interpretation, according to James and Lange. For starters, if you see a scary scene in a film and realize your heart is beginning to pound, James and Lange think you'll understand the physiological reaction (of your heart racing) as you're afraid. You assume then that you are afraid because your heart is pounding. The clinical hypothesis of fear James-Lange suggests that your heart is not pounding because you are afraid; instead, you are scared because your heart is racing. The feeling of terror that you experience at that point in time is therefore a reference to the physiological reaction that is taking place in your body.

The Cannon-Bard theory of emotion is another influential theory which seeks to explain the origin and essence of emotions. This is also a theory of physiology but it seeks to directly counter James and Lange's submissions.

This theory, proposed by Walter Cannon and further expanded by Philip Bard, explains that humans experience physiological reactions connected to certain emotions without necessarily experiencing those emotions. For example, when you do something exciting like exercise, your heart also races, like when you're afraid. People experience emotional responses so easily, according to Cannon, that they literally cannot be the results of some physical reactions. As an example, when you watch that scary movie scene, you often start feeling frightened even before you notice that your heart is racing or your hands are shaking. Essentially, Cannon and Bard claim that emotional responses and physiological reactions to internal or external stimuli frequently occur simultaneously.

The Schechter-Singer hypothesis is yet another relational philosophy that explores feelings from a theoretical viewpoint. According to this hypothesis, first human beings undergo a physiological reaction after which they seek to identify the cause of this reaction so that they can feel it as an emotion. In other words, you respond with a physiological response to external or internal stimuli, which you then perceive from a cognitive perspective; what is called an emotion is the product of the cognitive understanding. The Schechter and Singer theory is quite similar to both James-Lange and Cannon-Bard theory but the main difference, according to Schechter and Singer, is the semantic understanding that people use to mark a feeling.

Schechter and Singer have claimed, as did Cannon and Bard, that certain hormonal reactions in the body can result in different emotions.

Richard Lazarus has suggested the Lazarus Theory of Emotion or Cognitive Appraisal Theory as it is also known, and it is another theory that takes a cognitive approach. This theory suggests thought often takes place before feeling emotion. According to Lazarus and other pioneers of this theory, humans immediately react to stimuli with thoughts, after which they experience the physiological response and emotions. Which means your emotions often come first before an emotional and physiological reaction. For example, if you watch a scary scene in a film, your mind immediately starts to think this film is scary and scary. It induces an emotion of panic, followed by associated physical reactions like trembling hands, heart racing etc.

Ultimately, we have the subjective Facial-Feedback principle. This theory suggests that our facial expressions are related to the emotional experiences. What this means is that your physical reactions to stimuli have a direct impact on the emotion you are experiencing, rather than being the emotional effects. This hypothesis claims that our emotions are directly related to changes in the muscles of our heads. For starters, you'll have a better time at social events if you encourage yourself to smile more when interacting with people. And, if you're carrying a frown every time you interact with people at social events, you'd definitely feel a terrible emotion.

These are all moral hypotheses formulated by scholars over the years. You may ask why you even need to know about relational theory merely because you want to learn how to control your emotions. There's one key thing you need to do first to master your emotions; understand how the emotions occur. If you want to learn how to control an emotion like rage, the cause of the anger and all the symptoms associated with it will certainly be established first. Once you know that, the next time you feel it brewing, you can easily put a leash onto your rage.

Emotions are an integral part of our lives because they have tremendous effects on our attitudes, emotions, and decisions and eventually on our futures. There may still be a huge cloud of mystery surrounding why we experience emotions but we should be able to understand and control our emotions efficiently with the little information that we have available to us.

- **Anger**

Anger is one of the most unwelcome feelings, yet it still expresses itself. One cause of anger is when an individual feels that they are entitled to something. For example, if you feel you deserve an award, respect, and attention, then when you get disappointed you are on the path of attracting anger. Many people who tend to be temperamental often have a low self-esteem that means that every failure they receive makes them think they're destined to fail. Anger will cost your health, social life, jobs and livelihood if unmanaged.

- **Fear/Discomfort**

We get nervous every time we try something different. We worry about the unknown. So we like to maintain our daily routine and live inside our comfort zones. From the point of view of our minds, that makes perfect sense. If our current habits enable us to be safe and avoid any potential threat to our survival (or our ego's survival) why bother to change them? It is why we often maintain the same schedule, or often have the same feelings. It is also why when we try to change ourselves we can experience a lot of internal resistance.

- **Grief**

It's important to grieve someone's loss or something important in your life, but if it isn't managed correctly, grief can snowball into a debilitating emotion. If you are overcome with sadness, then try to be more patient. It is easy to withdraw socially while grieving, and to stop productive activities. Force yourself to engage with others and seek out from the people you're close to the emotional support you need. Don't let them stagnate your life. Continue your mindfulness, sleep, cook right and everything else that makes you feel good.

Understand that you need not feel guilty for going on from a defeat. Just because you have acknowledged the thing or person's absence does not mean that you have forgotten.

- **Happiness**

Happiness considers what we want to do in an appealing way as one of the most sought after emotions. At the personal, community, and governmental levels, there are numerous efforts and strategies to enhance levels of happiness as it directly impacts people's health. Happiness is expressed as an emotion by body languages such as a relaxed attitude, facial expressions such as laughing, and an optimism that is demonstrated by a friendly tone of voice.

The state of joy, like any other feeling, is primarily created by human experience and the belief system. For example, if scoring sixty marks is considered desirable, then a student will probably feel happy to attain or exceed the mark. If riding in a train with family members is considered happy then an individual who has never had that experience could feel happy and anxious about the prospect of boarding a train. Thankfully, we can maximize satisfaction by rising our levels of emotional intelligence.

- **Sadness**

Sadness, as an emotion, is a transient emotional state whose attributes include hopelessness, grief, deception, dampened mood and disinterest. There are several ways in which sadness can be manifested as emotion including:

- Withdrawal from others
- Dampened mood
- Lethargy
- Crying
- Quietness

- **Envy**

Envy commonly occurs at the workplace where an employee admires being accomplished just as the popular colleague does. A human is routinely entertaining and pursuing ambitions and this is allowed. The problem begins when one becomes dissatisfied with other's successes to the point of being mentally and physically affected; the individual is feeling envious. As expected, persons with a feeling of envy will rarely admit that the negative emotion is manifested. At the workplace, envy has a negative effect on a person. While the small and periodic source of envy is required to drive one on to develop and aspire for more, if it is not handled it becomes a problem. Envy feelings are likely to manifest commonly at work as workplaces appraise employees and reward those accomplished.

Overcoming jealousy means accepting that we have different skills and different timings. By accepting that there are more qualified individuals than you will help you create space to accept others to become more successful than you are. It is also important to note that experienced personnel are likely to deliver when opposed to newcomers. Unlearning ability can help in managing the feeling of envy. As with any sentiment, one can't escape feeling jealous, but one can handle the feeling effectively. When the feeling of jealousy sets in, reassure yourself that you will take the feeling off in one hour and not respond to a friend or colleague's achievement.

- **Anxiety**

To allow one to imagine and prepare for the worst-case scenarios, feeling worried is necessary. For example, being concerned about passing exams helps you to tackle the risk of failure by working harder, studying, or failure preparation as a possible outcome of the study you were taking. However when it takes over you, anxiety becomes a negative emotion and removes one from daily tasks and regular experiences. For example, if you are constantly worried about failure to study until you get burnout, then worry about it as emotion becomes a negative emotion. As indicated earlier, feelings emanate from human experience and belief system, and this implies that if the society fails to accommodate failure, then you will get an emotion of concern. Due to past experiences and the existing system of beliefs about tests, the feeling is manifesting and not really about how you feel inside.

- **Self-criticism**

Self-judgment occurs when we judge and consider ourselves lacking. As a way of self-evaluation, self-criticism is important and can help one develop results, social skills and communication. A fortunate aspect of human beings is that they can reflect on their experiences, detach themselves from themselves and assess themselves and speak to themselves. Limited self-assessment can help to increase personal accountability, which can increase an individual's professionalism and attractiveness at work and in society. Self-criticism, though, becomes an issue when one holds to it and feels worthless to society.

- **Frustration**

This is when you feel trapped but there is nothing you can do about it. On-the-job frustration is the most common burnout cause.

- **Worry**

It's normal to be worried about losing your job, with so many layoffs. Instead of feeling anxious, though, try to focus on your work and think of ways to improve your efficiency, to make you more employable. People who are nervous generally have low self-confidence.

- **Disappointment**

Repeated disappointments always have a negative effect on efficiency and productivity and can lead to burnout and high staff turnover if unaddressed.

The key thing about nurturing negative emotions in the workplace is that these feelings are contagious, and this kind of resentment easily spreads and demoralizes others, be it feelings about your colleagues, management, work environment, salary, or something else. This is why a pessimistic person is more likely to be shot, if for no other reason than to avoid spreading the anger and frustration to others.

Anger is often perceived from a primary emotional point of view but anger may also be a secondary emotion. Anger is, in reality, often more secondary than first. Anger is a basic human emotion which is linked to our human survival. It's as fundamental as happiness, sadness, fear and other basic emotions. Unlike stress and anxiety, rage is also associated with the nervous system's "fight or flight" response; it's intended for your safety and security. The response to combat or flight is usually activated when someone perceives danger; it prepares you either to fight or to flee from the perceived danger. Combating in this answer, however, has progressed from actual combat to other items. There are cases where "fighting" does not mean getting the punch ready; by championing a cause for justice, it may respond to an injustice.

Contrary to what you were led to think, indignation is a human emotion that is perfectly normal, typically healthy and natural. Yet, when it gets out of control, rage can become harmful too. At some point in time we all feel anger though in varying degrees. This is because the anger is a part of our human experiences. Anger usually occurs in different contexts, and is usually preceded by some emotions that could generally be pain, injustice, dissatisfaction, criticism, and unfairness. Anger usually comes in varying degrees from annoyance to fury. Anger in the form of mild irritation can be due to feelings of stress, fatigue and anxiety. In reality, human beings are likely to get frustrated when their basic human needs such as food, shelter, and sleep are not fulfilled. They may also get annoyed by other people's thoughts and beliefs that don't adhere to ours.

Often it becomes destructive when anger becomes an emotion which we cannot control. It can have a huge impact on our personal and working relationship with others, but this does not stop. Anger is also mentally, and emotionally damaging to our wellbeing. Usually stress occurs with unchecked anger and when anger is prolonged the stress hormones that come with anger can destroy certain neurons in some part of the brain that is responsible for short-term memory and judgment. Anger may weaken the immune system, as well.

As we have said, rage is a basic human emotion necessary for survival so there are occasions that anger can be good and not "evil." In reality, anger is not in itself a "bad" emotion; it gets bad when we allow it to get us uncontrolled, i.e. when it becomes uncontrollable. Every emotion is inherently bad as long as we are able to master those feelings and control them. Anger may be a substitute emotion sometimes used to cover up something like pain, envy, jealousy, and so on. There are people who get angry, just so that they don't have to feel pain. People often shift their feelings from pain to anger, because being mad is better than being in pain. That can be an event conscious or unconscious.

Anger is usually grouped by experts into several types and we will be checking out 8 types of anger identified for this book. Knowing the type or cause of your rage makes monitoring or manipulation of this frustration simpler. All forms of anger that we will analyze are mentally focused, because anger is a mind emotion.

- **Righteous Anger**

This is a positive anger we feel when an injustice was committed or when we feel that a rule was broken. It can also be called judgmental or hypocritical indignation because it is a morally indignant anger that can also occur because of our understanding of the shortcomings of someone else. Normally, this sort of anger comes from conviction and law. The rage you get when you suspect violation of someone's human right is a just indignation. Nonetheless, this kind of indignation might presume a morally superior mentality that is that you think you're better than some people and that's why you get upset at them; it may also be that you believe somebody is different than something they've done. Because of the need to manipulate and control others, just anger can become excessive.

• **Assertive Anger**

Have you ever used your feelings of rage to promote a favorable or beneficial change in society? If so, we're referring to this as assertive frustration. It's a constructive kind of anger that serves as a catalyst for initiating changes that aim to change the state of something positively. Instead of expressing anger in the form of confrontations, protests, outbursts and verbal abuse, individuals who become assertively angry express their anger in terms that create a positive shift around the situation that first made them angry. This is usually done without any sort of harm, anxiety or panic. Assertive anger can provide you with a really powerful motivator.

- **Aggressive Anger**

This type of anger is also called behavioral anger, and is usually expressed physically. It is a highly volatile, unpredictable, and out-of-control which can push you to attack someone physically. Nevertheless, that doesn't mean that rage necessarily leads to hurt or death. If this frustration overwhelms you, it may cause you to lash out at the source of your rage or something like the wall or a photo frame nearby. Aggressive or mental retribution can have significant civil and moral implications. The source of this form of rage can be abuse or childhood deprivation.

- **Habitual anger**

There are times when anger becomes a perpetual emotion, because you have been angry for so much time. Habitual anger refers to when you're in a constant state of irritation, dissatisfaction, and unrest that annoys you pretty much at all. Individuals with this kind of repetitive rage can get even more upset when they are faced with their frustration or some circumstances. The hidden reason behind this kind of resentment is that it is always profoundly rooted in the past and that it accumulates, perhaps due to negative interactions over the years. The older you get, the more you feed this anger, without managing it.

- **Chronic Anger**

This is a general type of rage, and dangerous. It is your situation's absolute and constant resentment, certain circumstances, people around you and even yourself. It is a form of normal frustration, because it is in perpetuity as well. Because it is an extended experience, chronic anger often has immensely adverse effects on the mental and physical wellbeing of an individual.

- **Passive-Aggressive Anger**

People who try to avoid confrontations and emotions are the ones who usually show the form of passive-aggressive rage. Passive-aggressive anger is about repressing your anger, rage, or fury to avoid arguments and confrontations. This frustration is often implicitly conveyed in the form of sarcasm, verbal abuse, ridicule, veiled silence and constant procrastination. Most people who passively express anger often do not accept being aggressive, but their actions may have harmful effects on their personal and professional relationship with others.

- **Verbal Anger**

Verbal rage is often considered milder than verbal or normal anger but it is just as severe. This rage is a fundamentally emotional and psychological one which has profound effects on the harassment target. It comes in the form of threats, mockery, sarcasm, shouting, screaming, shouting furiously, blaming and poor criticism. It's often experienced out of irritation or annoyance.

- **Self-harm**

This is a type of anger directed toward oneself. It goes much further than the depression. There are men, for instance, who cut themselves up; this could be expressing anger because they may not like their looks. Self-harm is pretty complicated though you should know it's a very negative emotion you can't hold in. So much can result in self-harm; physical abuse, emotional abuse, neglect and trauma. This may also be attributed to frequent disappointments. Instead of voicing their indignation to the person who wronged them, some people focus their frustration on their inner self.

No matter what type of rage you are feeling, there are certain triggers that are the main causes of frustration. You need to identify and address the cause of your anger in order for successful anger management to take place. So, let's take a look at some of the known anger causes.

Factors that Contribute to Anger

Apart from the fact that anger is a natural emotion you will feel, there are many factors that contribute to why you get angry. Whether you respond to circumstances depends on certain aspects in life, and the ones that decide the degree of frustration you have felt are these.

Your infancy and upbringing is the first known factor that contributes to how you experience anger. As children, certain beliefs about anger have been taught to many people; they have been taught that anger is destructive, evil and very negative. Individuals who were taught that expressing anger is bad learn not to complain about injustice; they might also have been punished for expressing their anger as children. So, they learn to keep the anger in, until it becomes a usual long-term issue. Occasionally, due to years of bottling all those feelings down, they end up showing their frustration in very unhealthy ways. If there are no other sources, they will turn the rage inwards too. There are also people who have grown up feeling it's OK to be aggressive or violent and they continue to violently carry out their rage. This may be because they have not been taught how to express or manage their emotions appropriately.

Another factor that contributes to anger is the past experiences you have had, and how you react to situations. As a teenager, if you have encountered circumstances that have led you to feel angry and resentful in the past but were unable to convey that frustration healthily at the moment, you may still be nurturing the rage until the present. For example, if you've been abused or faced a trauma in the past, the anger may still be lurking in your heart somewhere, especially if you weren't able to do anything about it then. It obviously results in you having certain circumstances that are particularly difficult and easy to get upset at.

Your anger issue may also be due to circumstances that you are currently facing, and not just things that you have experienced in the past. Current circumstances and challenges may leave you feeling angrier than normal, or may cause you to become angry with things and situations that are not even related. If there's a situation that makes you angry, and you can't do anything about it, you can express the anger in a completely different condition at other times. For example, if your boss at work makes you angry and stressed out every day but since he's your employer you can't do anything about it, you can show the frustration at home rather than at work. For starters, you can get home and lash grumpily or violently at the kids or your girlfriend, and then blame it on a "bad day." These are 3 of the most important reasons for what makes you upset and how you respond to potentially raging scenarios.

Anger as a Positive Emotion

As much as we all like to see anger as a negative emotion, it can also be a positive emotion when we react to it in the right way; it is also positive as long as we control our anger and never allow it to consume us. If anger is constructive it means that it pushes us to do something beneficial; positive anger lays the foundation for transformation and growth.

Positive anger is a highly motivating force that forces us to do something that we in the past might have thought we couldn't. Anger fuels our passion and drives us toward our goals regardless of the challenges and barriers that appear to stand in our way. It is a positive kind of feeling that infuses us with the requisite energy and motivation to get what we want; it can inspire a clamor for social change and justice (think Martin Luther King). Again it encourages us to be hopeful because frustration is a positive emotion. Now, you might find this strange and unlikely, but it's real. Just as joy does, Anger will make you hopeful.

Anger as a positive emotion can be of great benefit to our relationships too. It is a natural emotion and in our relationships, we have to try to be as natural as possible. There's no need to suck it in and repress your anger with a smile when you are wronged by your partner, relative or friend. Anger is destructive and harmful to a relationship when you ignore it, or conceal it, according to studies. If you repress your anger and give a false smile, you don't let your partner know what they've done to get you wrong so they can keep doing it that doesn't make the relationship good. However it strengthens your friendship and the bond you have with your partner as you express your frustration respectfully and healthily. Anger helps you find answers to any conflict you face in your relationship.

Anger can also be positive when we use it for self-consciousness; this emotion is a pretty good tool for ourselves to examine and look within. Anger helps us to see and reflect on our shortcomings. If you're never mad, there's every possibility you'd never realize what you're doing wrong for people to get the response that's causing your anger. Sometimes you are to blame and not the person who made you angry. You will discover ways to channel your frustration and change your life for the better when you become self-conscious and self-conscious. Meaningful indignation encourages positive change in one's self.

Okay, this next one sounds quite odd but what if you've learned that anger is reducing violence? Indeed, it absolutely does. We all know that anger is an emotion known to precede violence, so how can anger reduce violence even further? That happens is that when you get upset it can be a strong sign that shows you something has to be modified or fixed. When you notice this, you may be motivated by anger to take action to mediate the situation that could induce violence if not checked. Take a moment and imagine a world in which no one would automatically respond with outrage to injustice? Yeah, it seems like a mighty violent world. Often, when someone wrongs us and we show our indignation in a healthy manner, it can encourage them to take action and placate us and fix the wrong they have done.

Positive anger can actually be used to get what you want. However, one thing you should always keep in mind is that anger can only be used positively or positively when justifiable. Anger that makes you feel control is not positive and cannot be used to initiate positive or change developments. This is the kind of anger that you will need about the anger management techniques that we're going to discuss. Techniques for managing anger teach you to turn your anger from positive to negative.

Emotions and Your Mind

Your mind is special. There is no other psychological framework like yours, and emotions will be experienced differently from anyone else. Take one example of falling in love. This may feel like weightlessness / lightness or it may feel like trapping a million bees inside your stomach. It can be intense or it could be subtle. It may be sudden, or it may slowly appear. Anger, frustration, weariness and even happiness are the same. Just because you may not feel the same feeling in the same fashion as someone else does not devalue what you experience.

As no two people will experience the same emotion, no definition will be appropriate for each person in the same way. Two people struggling with depression, for example, will have very different symptoms. The former may have trouble sleeping, have no appetite, and have no interest in things that once were fun while the latter may have trouble sleeping in too long, binge-eating, and extreme waves of depression. These two instances of depression will look strikingly different from an outside viewer, but both emotions and experiences of these sufferers are valid and could be identified as depression.

This is why intense emotions such as grief have such disparate effects on different people. For example, two siblings face a parent's death, each one will deal with it in his or her own way. The former will cling to family and friends to help cope with the extreme pain, while the latter may become the family clown, cracking jokes to keep others laughing while coping with private sorrow. None of those responses are wrong; they are just different.

The trick is to stop comparing your emotional self with someone else's emotional selves. Identifying and describing one's feelings must be an internal affair. If we equate ourselves with others, we end up invalidating our feelings because they do not seem to' compete with what everyone else does.' The emotions are yours, and they are already true in the way that you perceive them.

Each time we feel not every feeling at the same level, by which I mean emotional intensity, changes according to what the experience is. For example, after hearing the news that a favorite performer has passed away, you may experience a low-intensity grief but you may experience a much fuller, more intense grief at a friend or relative's loss.

These are often constructive, as low-and mild-intensity emotions tend to be easier to cope with. You can weep over the loss of that favorite star but these cries are likely to be cathartic, bringing inner comfort through the emotional expression. On the other hand, a high-intensity emotion can be harder to face or cope with, causing both emotional and psychological distress. For example, a friend's death will cause that much higher intensity of sorrow, making it difficult to go on with everyday life.

Not everyone feels the same strength of the feelings. Some of us are meant to just feel more intensely than others. If you've ever found yourself overcome with emotion about what was a mundane situation for others, then you might be an intense feeler. This is not a bad thing, because it also means that you feel more intensely positive emotions, but being an intense feeling may be the reason you are struggling with emotions that are not managed properly. The higher the intensity, the harder it is to cope with the emotions.

Let's just take depression as an example. At some point in our lives we all feel grief because we are all coping with disappointment and loss, but a crippling and dangerous feeling is intense, high-intensity depression. It is natural and normal to become sad after a disappointment or a tragic event, but this typically does not alter our general perceptions and thought patterns. We face temporary sadness and then move on with life. Depression is not that easy to surmount. It is an emotion of high intensity that can seriously affect emotions, attitudes, and actions, sometimes without any apparent cause. Coping with sadness is a chore that is difficult but manageable whilst coping with depression is a long and complicated journey.

The Nature of Emotions

Emotions can be difficult. By understanding the mechanism behind the emotions, as they arise, you will be able to manage them more effectively.

The first thing you need to understand is the emotions come and go. You feel happy one moment, and sad the next. Although you have some power of your feelings, you have to understand their unpredictable nature as well. If you're going to be happy all the time, then you're setting up to fail. You then run the risk of blaming yourself if you' fail' to be happy, or even worse, beat up for it.

To begin taking control of your emotions, you have to accept that they are transitory. You must learn to let them pass without feeling the necessity of strongly identifying with them. You need to let yourself feel sad without adding comments like, "I shouldn't be upset," or "What's wrong with me?" You have to let reality be, instead.

Usually this is intended to be taken in a negative light when someone is identified as emotional. Emotional people are often perceived to be impulsive, hard to talk to, hard to work with, unscientific, emotional, disruptive or prone to being spoken to. But that characterization is based on emotional people's assumptions. Indeed, labeling someone as emotional is a simple and almost devious way of neutralizing and invalidating someone by labeling them immediately as something they might or might not be.

No matter how emotionally strong you are, preferably not at the same time, and not constantly, you will still feel sorrow, disappointment, or depression in your life. You'll also feel disappointed, hurt, insecure, resentful or embarrassed. You are going to doubt yourself and doubt your capacity to be the guy you want to be. But that's all right because feelings are coming yet, most specifically, they are going away.

WHERE DO EMOTIONS LIVE?

We are completely in contact with our emotional core, as babies and young children. We know what we hear... and that is very clear.

Consider about a young child— their feelings are often primal, intense and clear. Give the sugar to a child and they're feeling happiness! Take away the candy and they get rage, hurt or even fear.

Young baby mothers learn-babies will immediately pick up facial expressions and vocal speech. When it comes to feelings, they are very intuitive, because they just begin to grasp and appreciate them. We haven't learnt to "talk" like adults yet.

In fact, mothers were given instructions in one Harvard study to display no feelings or stare blankly at their baby for one minute. The babies had shown frustration at first. We tried to imitate the face of their mother. They only grinned, chuckled, and cooed, trying to get their mother's warm response. But the babies soon detected that something was wrong and the lack of reaction from Mom led them to experience fear. Incapable of picking up on what Mom expressed and thinking left them feeling very insecure and angry. Babies in the sample were all in full meltdown mode within just one minute or less.

The writers then have done the opposite. Mom was able to comfort the boy, and immediately reassured and content the baby. The babies sensed the bond and were sated as soon as mom could express emotion.

Sadly we are struggling to hold back our feelings as we grow up. We know that being too angry is not OK. How many of us, "Don't be so angry" or "Don't get so upset about it" have been told?

thoughts that you experience during this period. Of course, if you stop focusing on the intense emotion and the negative thoughts it triggers and turn your attention to questions in order to find a way out of the problem, you gently soothe your negative thinking process.

- Evaluate the whole issue in detail, then consider ways to solve the problem better. You easily overcome negative thoughts and create room for opportunities as you concentrate on the answer and not the problem.

It will be hard not to react to a strong emotion, but if you remain aware of how you feel and behave, and make consistent efforts, you will gradually nurture the habit of responding to your emotions, which will only help you to become more positive.

List of Different emotions

Generally feelings can be divided into two distinct types. These types, however, come in various forms. Many researchers divide emotions into two types: communicating emotions and regulating emotions. Others categorize emotions as: primary and secondary. One aspect that is similar in both emotional classifications. But are all types of feelings typically either positive or negative? It will be either negative or positive, whether an emotion is primary / secondary or expressed /

controlled. People often believe that positive psychology is mainly focused on positive emotions, but that's not entirely true. Of reality, positive psychology tends more towards negative emotions, because to produce positive results, it is more about controlling and overturning negative emotions.

Secondly, positive emotions can be described as emotions that give a pleasurable experience; they pleasure you and do not unhealthily affect your body. As expected, positive emotions foster positive self-development. Basically, we're saying that positive emotions are the result of pleasant responses to stimuli in or within the environment. Negative emotions, on the other hand, refer to those emotions that we do not find particularly pleasant, pleasurable or delightful to experience. Negative emotions are usually the result of unfavorable stimulus responses which cause us to convey a negative effect on a person or circumstance.

In reality we have different examples of classes of feelings under both positive and negative. Yet most of the time, if the feeling is positive or negative, you can not say authoritatively. There are, in reality, some emotions which could be both positive and negative. Use your intuition to discern between a positive and a negative emotion. Anger, for example, can be both positive and negative. So, the best way to know when it's negative or positive is to discern intuitively the cause and the context of the anger.

There has been substantial evidence based on research done in the past to prove that suppressing anger can be the precursor to cancer development in the body and can also inhibit progress even after the cancer has been diagnosed and treated.

Anger could have so many effects on your health. Let's dig at some of those impacts.

- **Heart Problems**

Anger places you at great risk of a heart attack. If you have an eruption of rage the risk of having a heart attack doubles. If you block or show your frustration through an unhealthy means, the effect goes straight to your heart, suggesting it may cause heart attacks. In fact, a study has shown that people with anger disorders or volatile anger are more likely than people with fewer signs of anger to have coronary illness. Nevertheless, constructive or positive anger is in no way connected with any heart problem. It could be very good for your health, too.

- **Weak Immune System**

In fact, getting angry all the time can weaken the immune system, making you prone to more and more diseases, as confirmed by a study. An angry outburst can cause a 6-hour reduction in the amount of immunoglobulin A, an antibody responsible for defending the body against infections, based on a study carried out at Harvard Medical School. Now imagine if you're always angry; if you don't learn to control your anger, you could really damage your immune system.

- **Cause Stroke**

If you are the sort that bursts every time, you're at a very high risk of having a severe stroke. Volatile and normal anger increases your chance of having a stroke anywhere from a potentially minor blood clot to the brain to actual brain bleeding.

- **Increase Anxiety**

It's natural to experience anxiety at one stage or the other but frustration will actually worsen the anxiety if caution is not taken. Anger is actually a primary emotion to anxiety, i.e. your anxiety may be due to the underlying anger problems. Anger raises Generalized Anxiety Disorder (GAD) symptoms which is an extreme case of anxiety. People with GAD have higher levels of repressed, internalized, and unspoken anger that contributes to the development of GAD symptoms; this can be quite destructive.

- **Causes Depression**

Anger increases anxiety that in turn can lead to clinical depression. Over the years, a lot of studies have found a connection between frustration, anxiety, and depression, particularly when men are involved. One of the symptoms of depression is passive frustration; you are constantly angry but too unmotivated to act on the anger.

- **Decreases Lifespan**

Anger causes stress and stress when it comes to ill health, is a very strong suspect. Anger can have a really strong effect on your health when combined with stress, and it can shorten your lifespan due to the number of health problems it can generate. People who experience constantly repressed anger have shorter lifespans than people who express their anger in a healthy way.

Anger should never be repressed, or expressed unhealthily. Instead, you should make active efforts to manage and control your anger to avoid all the negative effects of anger you've just learned about. You should never try to appease or block your rage. Suppressing emotions as we reiterated over the chapters makes it difficult to manage them or master them as you ought.

To begin with, pay attention to any feeling of rage that you encounter and use the information gained to determine where the frustration comes from, so that you can use one or more of the anger management strategies that we will point out below to successfully counter anger issues.

WHAT IS DARK PSYCHOLOGY?

Dark Psychology is the study of the human condition as it refers to people's psychological intent of preying on others. Humanity as a whole has an ability to victimize certain human beings & living creatures. While this tendency is restrained or sublimated by many, some act upon these impulses. Dark Psychology seeks to understand the emotions, feelings and beliefs that contribute to the actions of human predators. Dark Psychology assumes this production is purposive and 99.99 percent of the time has some rational, goal-oriented motivation. Under Dark Psychology, the remaining .01 percent is the brutal victimization of others without purposeful intent or reasonably defined by evolutionary science or religious dogma.

Benefits Of Knowing Your Dark Side

- How critique of others is often a defense mechanism, you become. We occasionally accuse others of our own shortcomings.
- Consider how your expressions often mask fear and anxiety, jealousy and envy
- You are conscious of your worries and anxieties
- Better understand our interactions with others
- Completely accept ourselves
- Freeing shame

Six Steps To Change Thought

- Make sure a person doesn't know something unusual is happening.
- Creates an entirely manipulated and isolated physical and social setting.
- Make the exploited person feel helpless
- Use punishment and incentive to disassociate the victim from previous behavior and lifestyle
- Use reward and punishment to make the group and its values look highly attractive
- Exercise absolute authority over the individual controlled by the cult.

CHAPTER 3

WHAT RULES YOUR EMOTIONS?

Emotions from individuals, locations, and times of the day or even certain objects can be caused by all sorts of things. What stimuli function is to stimulate our brain's emotions or memories, which allow us to have physical and emotional responses.

Having emotions is a normal human reaction to the circumstances of our lives, the problem comes when we cannot assess our emotions or consider their impact on our lives. Most people accept their emotions passively; they don't even get to the points that we've covered where they choose to identify what the emotion is or what triggered it.

How Our Thoughts Shape Our Emotions

Walter Mischel, social psychologist, led numerous psychological studies on deferred compensation and pleasure during the 1960s. He observed closely hundreds of children between the ages of 4 and 5 years to discover a characteristic that is considered to be one of the most important factors influencing a person's life achievement, satisfaction.

This experiment is known as the Marshmallow test. The procedure involved the entrance of each infant into a private chamber and the positioning of a single marshmallow before them. The researcher made a deal with the child at this point.

We were told by the researcher that he would have left the chamber for some time. The kid was then told that if he or she did not eat the marshmallow while the researcher was gone, he would come back and compensate them separately from the one on the table with an extra marshmallow. When they did eat the marshmallow set in front of them on the counter, though, they wouldn't be rewarded with another.

It was simple. An instant marshmallow, or two subsequent marshmallows.

The researcher walked out of the chamber and after 15 minutes entered again.

Predictably, some kids leaped in front of them on the marshmallow, then ate it as soon as the researcher left the room. Though, by diverting their attention, some tried hard to contain themselves. In a bid to stop them from chewing the marshmallow, they hopped, skipped around and scooted on the seats to confuse themselves. Many of these kids, however, did not resist the temptation and finally gave up.

Only a handful of kids managed to hold out without eating the marshmallow until the very end.

The study was published in 1972 and became popular worldwide as' The Marshmallow Experiment.' It doesn't end here though. What followed several years later, is the real twist in the tale.

Investigators conducted a follow-up analysis to track each child's life and development that was a part of the initial trial. We researched many aspects of the life of the person and were taken aback by what we found. The kids who deferred pleasure for higher rewards or waited until the end to win two marshmallows instead of one had higher school grades, fewer substance abuse incidents, reduced risk of obesity and improved ability to cope with stress.

The work became regarded as a ground-breaking analysis on gratification as researchers followed up on the children 40 years after the original experiment was performed, and it was fairly clear that the group of children who diligently deferred gratification for higher rewards were competitive in all aspects on which they were assessed.

This analysis showed without doubt that delaying gratification is one of the most critical life-long abilities for success.

Success and delaying gratification

Success usually boils down to picking up on the fun and ease of relaxation between the pain of discipline. It is precisely that which is slowing satisfaction. Do you want to go out for the new film in the area where all your buddies are going, or would you prefer to sit up and study for an exam to earn good grades? Would you rather have a fun party with your friends before the team starts with an important meeting coming up? Or are you going to sit back late and focus on fine tuning the presentation?

Our ability to delay gratification is also a major factor in decision-making and is regarded as an important aspect of emotional intelligence. We make many choices and decisions each day. While some of them are insignificant and have little effect on our life (what color shoes will I buy? or how should I get to work?), others have a huge impact on our progress and potential.

We are programmed, as human beings, to make decisions or choices that give an immediate return on investment. We want the performance, behaviors and incentives to be quick. Obviously the mind is geared to a short-term profit. Why do you think the e-commerce companies do a killing by paying an additional fee for distribution the same day and the next day? It's better today, than tomorrow!

What about how different our life would be if we knew about the three to five years from now effect of our decisions? If we can bring about this mental shift where fulfillment can be postponed by having our sights firmly fixed on the larger picture many years from now, our lives can be quite different.

The important factor in delayed gratification is the climate. For starters, because children who have been able to resist disappointment have not been given a second marshmallow or a reward of delaying gratification, they are less likely to consider delaying gratification as a good habit.

When parents fail to maintain their willingness to compensate a child for delaying gratification, the child will not respect the quality. Only in an environment of commitment and trust, where a second marshmallow is given when deserved, can the delaying gratification be taken up.

Examples of gratification delay

Let us say you want to buy your dream car that you see every day on your way to work in the showroom. You imagine how wonderful it would be to own this car and to drive it. The car costs $25,000, and your current savings are barely $5,000 dollars. How then do you buy the car? Easy, you get to save. This is how you combine powerful will with delayed gratification.

There are countless opportunities for you to blow money every day, like hitting the bar on weekends with friends for a drink, visiting the nearest coffee shop to grab a latte or buying expensive gadgets. You have two clear choices each time you empty your wallet to pay: either blow up your money for physical gratification or wait for the long-term payout. If you can withstand these temptations and cut back on your expenses, you will be closer to buying your dream car. Taking that decision will allow you in the future to purchase something highly desirable.

Will you spend on instant gratifications and rewards today, or will you save on doing something more valuable in the future?

Here is another interesting example where the concept of delayed gratification can be explained. Let's say you want to be the world's best movie director ever seen. You want to master the craft and take all the skills related to film making and entertainment. You see yourself as making amazing films that have been empowering and entertaining people for decades.

How do you plan to work towards a big goal, or (well, literally) the big picture? You're going to start by doing mundane, boring; uninspiring jobs on the sets like being someone's assistant, getting them a cup of coffee, cleaning the sets and other similar boring chores. It's not thrilling or enjoyable, but every day you go through it because you've got your sights firmly fixed on the bigger goal, or the bigger picture.

You know that one day you want to become a major filmmaker and are willing to delay gratification in achieving that goal. Compared to the pleasure of the higher objective, the discomfort of your present life is smaller. That is pleasure deferred. Despite the discomfort, you are regulating your actions and behavior to achieve a larger future goal. Now it may be rough and tedious, but you know that doing such arduous jobs will give you your chance to make it big someday.

Delayed gratification from health to relationships can be applicable in all aspects of life. Almost every decision we make involves a choice between now opting for short-term pleasures and later enjoying greater rewards. Today, a burger can give you immediate pleasure, while an apple may not give you instant pleasure but in the long run it will benefit your body.

Stop drop technique

Each time you identify an overpowering or stressful emotion that is compelling you to seek immediate pleasure, describe your feelings by writing them down. Make sure you state them clearly to acknowledge their existence.

Did you see versions of old VCRs? They had a big pause button positioned prominently in the middle. Now you will press the pause button to your feelings.

Concentrate all attention on your heart as it is the center of all your feelings.

Think of a remarkably beautiful thing that you have experienced. It can be a stunning sunset that you've seen on one of your journeys, a gorgeous flower that you've seen in a garden today, or an adorable little kitten that you've seen nearby. Generally anything that evokes in your feelings of joy, happiness and positivity. The intention is to trigger a change in your emotions.

Experience the feeling for a while, and let it linger. Imagine the feelings that you feel within and around your heart. If still challenging, take breaths deep. Hold the feeling positive, and enjoy it.

Now, press the Psychological Pause button and explore the convincing thought that triggered feelings of tension. How's he feeling right now?

So write down how you felt and what you think comes to mind. Respond on the fresh insight when necessary.

This process doesn't take much time (again, you want instant gratification) and makes it easier for you to resist the temptation of giving in. The real trick is to alter with the heart the physical feeling to bring about a difference in thoughts and ultimately actions. You're not suffocating or stifling your feelings.

Instead, you acknowledge them and then change them gently. Then your emotions change slowly, the brain towers its line that makes us think in a way that allows us to act in accordance with our values and not on impulse or uncontrollable emotions.

Self-mastery is the master key

According to Walter Mischel, "Goal-directed and self-imposed reward delay is central to the mechanism of emotional self-regulation." The idea of emotional intelligence is essential to emotional awareness, or regulation, and the ability to control one's urges.

Mischel's research found that while some people are born with stronger impulse control, or better emotional regulation, others are not. There is a majority of people somewhere in between. The good news though is that, unlike intelligence, emotional management can be learned through practice. EQ is not determined genetically as are executive skills.

Impulse control and delayed gratification

Have you ever said anything in anger and then immediately regretted it? Have you ever pushed or hurried to regret it shortly after the act? I can't even count the number of people who lost their jobs, ruined their marriages, nixed up their business deals and blown away connections because of that one moment where they acted on impulses. You show low emotional intelligence when you do not allow thought to take over and control your words or actions.

The concept of emotional intelligence is thus closely related to the delaying gratification. At one point or another we've all acted without worrying about the consequences of our actions. Impulse control is a huge part of emotional control, or the ability to construct our thoughts and actions before we speak or act. When you learn to override impulses, you can manage your emotions more efficiently, which is why pulse control is a huge part of emotional intelligence.

Have you ever wondered why you count to ten, 100, or 1000 before you respond every time you're angry? We've all had advice from our parents and educators on how to restrain anger by counting as much as ten or 100. While you are in the process of counting it is simple; your emotional level is slowly declining. The overpowering impulse for reacting to the emotion has passed once you're done with counting. This allows you to act more rationally and with more thought.

The purpose of emotional intelligence is to identify and regulate these impulsive reactions more positively and constructively. Instead of being mindlessly responding to a situation, you need to stop and think before you answer. Instead of responding impulsively you choose to adapt cautiously to achieve a more positive outcome or thwart a potentially uncomfortable situation.

Here are some useful tips to postpone satisfaction and to improve the ability to control emotions:

- **Have a clear vision for your future**

It's better to postpone pleasure and regulate urges or thoughts when you have a good picture of the future. If you know what you want to accomplish in five, eight, ten, or fifteen years from now, keeping the bigger picture in mind will be much easier if you encounter temptations that can ruin your objective. Your' why' (compelling reason for achieving a goal) will keep you focused throughout the goal-fulfillment process. Once you have a specific goal in mind, prepare to achieve that goal. Identifying your goals and planning how you'll get there will help you more effectively withstand the temptation.

- **Find ways to distract yourself from temptations and eliminate triggers**

For example, if you intend to quit drinking, if there are several bars along the way, take a different route back home from work. Rather than dwelling on what you can't do, concentrate on the things you're excited about. Surround yourself with positive people and activities to help you remain on track. Stop wasting your day with material goods.

- **Make spending money difficult**

If you're a slave to plastic money and online transactions, you make it too easy to spend money for your own good. Hard cash payments will make you think many times before you invest. When you pay with real money rather than plastic you will reconsider your purchases. Take a portion of your paycheck and put it in a separate account you will not be handling. Make sure your savings account is not easy to access.

- **Avoid 'all or nothing' thinking**

Most of us believe that avoiding addiction or giving up a bad habit is an' all or nothing struggle.' Here and there, it's common for a lot of normal people to have a minor slip. That doesn't mean you should just drop off and quit, though. You should not use occasional slip-ups as an excuse to get off the track. You can get back onto the track despite a small detour. Don't try to persuade yourself to go the other way round.

- **Make a list of common rationalizations**

Find each one a counterpoint or counter-argument. You've just been angry for five minutes, for example, or you're spending just ten dollars extra. Tell yourself that five minutes of anger is wasted in anger for 150 minutes a month, or ten extra dollars is $3,000 spent all year round.

HOW TO REDUCE ANXIETY

1. Stay in your time zone.

Anxiety is a state of mind that is geared to the unknown. And turn yourself back to the present instead of thinking about what is going to happen. Ask yourself: What's going on right now? Am I safe? Do I need to do it right now? If not, make an "appointment" to check in with yourself later in the day to discuss your questions so you won't be knocked off course by those remote scenarios.

2. Relabel what's happening.

Sometimes panic attacks will lead you to feel like you are dying or having a heart attack. Remember: "I'm having a panic attack, but it's innocuous, it's brief, and there's nothing I need to do," Also, bear in mind that it's actually the opposite of a sign of impending death— the body is triggering its fight-or-flight reflex, the mechanism that will keep you alive.

3. Fact-check your thoughts.

Think about how practical they are in overcoming those issues. Say you are uncomfortable at a presentation of a big job. Instead of saying, for example, "I'm going to bomb," say, "I'm nervous but I'm prepared. Some events will go well and some may not. "Going into a habit of reconsidering the anxieties helps train your brain and find a reasonable way to deal with your anxious thoughts.

4. Breathe in and out.

Deep respiration helps calm you down. While you may have learned of different breathing exercises, there's no need to think about counting a number of breaths out. Instead only focus on inhaling and exhaling equally. That will help to slow down the thinking and re-center it.

CHAPTER 4

FACTORS AFFECTING EMOTIONS AND YOUR MOOD

What impacts emotions? This is a valid question to ask if you wish to understand your emotions and master them. They would look at two crucial things that impact emotions from the perspective of this chapter; the brain and social norms / community.

The brain is a great master of manipulating emotions so it could be really tricky even if you think you know the source of your feelings or emotions. They like to believe that our emotions and the reasons behind these feelings are in order, but the fact is that our subconscious has a much greater influence than we like to admit.

There are lots of activities going on in your head every single moment and the brain is at the core of all those tasks and somewhat complicated processes. There's a lot of process involved with how we interpret and react to situations. Remember the three important things characterize emotions: awareness, responses and response. The brain decides the thing that makes us wonder if our brain is actually affecting our emotions. What happens right in your brain when you feel an emotion?

The first thing you need to know about your emotions is that they start right from your head. Emotions are a combination of our feelings, the way these feelings are processed and our responses or reactions to those feelings. According to Charles Darwin the primary purpose of emotion is to encourage seamless human evolution. We have to pass on our genetic information from generation to generation in order for us to survive, which is why emotions are significant. Recognizing the importance of emotional experiences, the brain takes upon itself the task of assessing stimuli and triggering an appropriate emotional response. The brain reflects and considers the best way to react to a situation in order to achieve the primary purpose of survival, and then activates an appropriate emotion as a response to propel the rest of the body to react accordingly. And, when you find yourself responding to a situation with some kind of reaction, that's basically your brain activating the emotion it deems right at that moment in time for your safety.

The brain is an extensive network of complex processes that include information processing. One of the main neural networks includes neurons that send signals from some part of the brain to another. So, through what we call neurotransmitters, these cells or neurons send signals; some kind of chemicals we either absorb or discharge into the brain. The neurotransmitters are what cause one part of the brain to interact with another. Dopamine, norepinephrine, and serotonin are among the neurotransmitters that have been widely studied. Dopamine is the neurotransmitter that has to do with pleasure and rewards feelings; it's the chemicals that make you happy when you do something good. This neurotransmitter is released to give you a pleasant and happy feeling as a reward. In comparison, serotonin is the neurotransmitter associated with learning and memory. Regeneration of brain cells is known to play a critical role, and research has shown that a serotonin imbalance can lead to increased stress, frustration, anxiety and depression. Norepinephrine alone helps modify your moods by controlling the stress and anxiety levels.

So, when there is an unexpected or unbalanced release and absorption of either of these substances, the thoughts and emotional state are typically very deeply impacted. For example, if you do something that needs dopamine to be released and sent to the part of the brain that is responsible of information processing because your brain is not storing or absorbing the dopamine as it should, it could lead you to feel sad or mildly upset. The irregular production and distribution of dopamine, serotonin, and norepinephrine therefore has an immense impact on the feelings you have and the reactions you provide to certain conditions. These neurotransmitters remember the next time something that should have made you happy causes you feelings of sadness.

Your brain again exerts emotional influence because it's central to how emotions are formed. The brain consists of various parts all of which are responsible for generating different emotions. The part of the brain responsible for emotion processing is the' emotional brain' which is generally called the limbic system. We have the amygdala in this limbic system where, as we said in a previous chapter, lets you assess the emotional intensity or meaning of a stimulus before activating an appropriate response; it is the part of the brain which is responsible for initiating the response to fight or flight. The hypothalamus helps regulate the response to emotional triggers or reactions. Other parts of the brain, such as the hippocampus, also affect your emotions because of their memory recovery functions. The hippocampus ultimately decides the emotional responses to the stimuli. Because different parts of the brain process different types of emotions using different methods, injury to any part of the brain will change the emotions and moods considerably no matter how mild. The limbic system that adopts a generalized and simplistic response to sensations is central to all of this.

The left and right hemispheres of the brain both play important roles in emotion and reactions. The hemispheres are responsible for keeping you working but they also play a part in how information is processed. The left hemisphere treats concrete thinking more while the right hemisphere focuses on abstract thinking. The left and right hemispheres work together to control feelings because they both process information in different ways. Though an emotion is identified by the right hemisphere, the left hemisphere interprets the emotion. For example, when the right part of the brain identifies an emotion as anger, it alerts the left brain, which then makes a logical decision to interpret the emotional context and decide on the appropriate response to be given. Obviously this is all a coordinated device, but if something goes wrong and one hemisphere is unable to do its job properly, it will influence how you respond to basic emotions. For instance, if the right brain doesn't recognize a negative emotion as it should, it causes the left brain to get confused by the emotion without understanding how to react.

Memory whether the function of the brain is long-term or short-term and our memories dictate our emotions and inform them. Once you recall a resentful memory, you get furious and relaxed once you remember a fun memory. This is an ongoing process within the brain; it detects a previous feeling and then puts you in an emotion-based state. So when you get angry next without knowing why, it may be that your brain will recall some painful memory to start a negative emotion. How you can override that is to push yourself to think about things that in the past made you happy. For example, if you're depressed, simply thinking about some happy memories will trigger the release of dopamine that provides you with positive feelings.

- **Sleep**

When do you struggle with sleep the most? It's probably the times you've had so much in your mind and it seemed like rest was a far-fetched idea. Anxiety and negative emotions can make a person anxious and this has adverse effects on the rhythms of sleep.

Quality sleep is one of the prerequisites for a healthy body and it can cause a ripple effect when the body is deprived of sleep that will affect you both mentally and physically. Loss of sleep can affect your attention span. With time, you will find that you are not paying enough attention to your job, or what others are talking about you.

Sleep deprivation also stops the body from strengthening the immune system with the cytokines required for infection control. If you don't have enough cytokine in your body, you'll need a longer time to recover from illness.

Some of the negative emotions that affect your ability to sleep comfortably everyday are anxiety, stress, terror, panic attacks and depression. If you don't find a way to handle these emotions, you'll face more troublesome mental and physical problems.

- **Sports**

Over a series of studies this has been proved true. So if you want to keep your thoughts under control, stay away from junk food, eat balanced meals, and maintain a good exercise routine.

It can be tough to keep your emotions in check-overtime. This is why a lot of people do not make a lot of effort and eventually give up. Occasionally you lose the plot, but that shouldn't dissuade you from continuing on.

A person who is able to manage his emotions effectively and put his feelings under control will be seen as one with logical reasoning, an effective conflict handler, a person with high emotional intelligence, inner peace and self-confidence.

- **Food and drinks**

When a person is struggling with negative emotions, the last thing on their mind is usually food. In that state no eating may or may not be intentional. But anxiety always paves the way for eating disorders and this is true because in the past most people who are diagnosed with eating disorders struggle or may have faced stress.

Food disorders are diseases. The people who experience them notice in food a sudden change that is usually caused by their fear over weight gain and how they feel.

- **Music**

Art is a great way to use nonverbal speech to improve the well-being of the mind. Art is a magical carrier of human emotion; we tend to use art to comprehend and make sense of the world. Nevertheless, this is not the art's sole function; there are many roles. One is dancing; others are relaxing, grieving, mourning, celebrating, and stirring up war. There are a lot of music roles and almost all of them are our feelings.

Music is a great example of an art form in which subjective perception can be changed and emotional understanding brought on. If a person is sad all day, and goes to work, gets home, eats dinner, and watches a movie before going to bed, without any other consideration, they just keep that sadness within. To deal with emotions you have to do something about it, and learning to deal with emotions only taught after a person is able to recognize their feelings is the first step on the path to self-realization.

- **Relationships**

You are ready to work on improving your relationships once you have improved your social awareness skills and understood how to understand what others are thinking. Let's make it clear from the beginning- it's not an easy job. All other areas of emotional intelligence will need to be used to help you build and maintain them.

Four Things You Need to Know

The first thing that you need to evaluate and manage is the effect that different people have on you, as well as recognizing what they feel and what is the cause they feel that way. If you do that, you will be able to make a decision on how best to connect with them in order to achieve the outcome that fits your needs or their needs.

The effectiveness of the relationship management is determined by four different criteria:

- Deciding which course of action is best suited to a given situation. To understand that, you'll need to identify the other party's current mood and the explanation for that emotion. You'll obviously have multiple choices to communicate based on the research you've done, and each of them will trigger a different response. You will also recognize the effect they have on you and manage it appropriately
- Interacting with the other party based on your research
- The result is what should guide you to choose what to say and how to communicate your message. This means your actions come with a common goal in mind, making it a deliberate task to control your relationship
- Your desires are what will lead you to want a particular outcome. It could be your own personal needs or your business needs

Seven Competencies

Most talents can better be related to relationships in the industry but they can also be applied to relationships outside the workplace. The reason you should connect them directly to your office is because they have a lot of similarities with lawmakers.

Goleman described the skills, including:

- Influencing – the ability to persuade other people into doing something that suits your, their, or mutual desires
- Motivating – the capability to inspire many people by motivating them
- Developing – the ability to give useful feedback to support others develop their knowledge and skills
- Being a catalyst for change – recognizing what change is needed and initiating a cycle
- Conflict management – willingness to resolve or disagree quickly, differences of opinion or disagreements
- Team formation – networking and maintaining
- Working with others – building and cultivating successful teams

You can use every of these abilities to sustain your relationships. Before you do that, though, take some time to reflect on them.

The question you should ask yourself is "Do you implement these skills right now, and are you good at them?" Writing everything down is always a good idea. Think about different areas of each skill, and note what you're doing well and what can be improved. For example, giving other people feedback is something you are sure to do right now. On the other hand, you can also write where you could use some enhancement (yes, this could be the same ability, just another area).

The next move is to talk of two steps you will be taking to improve yourself and write them down in that area. They all include taking an online course, conducting your own research, reading a book or trying to mirror someone you respect. Eventually, try to actually carry out those acts and focus on your skills. You'll notice it improves the management of your relationships with others.

Let's take a look at the feedback give example. You're giving it to other people now but you'd like to focus on it and make it more helpful. You conduct an online research and find out some tips and try to apply them when someone asks you for feedback next time you do. You will notice that they will appreciate the feedback that is supportive and constructive, and thereby benefit your relationship.

Work environment

Due to the nature of human interactions and the need to take risks, as well as adventure, it is not possible to eliminate all difficult situations for emphasis. External factors, however, are beyond the reach of individual control. Among the effective ways to condition the mind to handle setbacks is to avoid circumstances which trigger adverse emotions. An example of this is where an individual feels frustrated when a deadline approaches rapidly. It could help if the person began planning and working earlier by dividing the work into modules. Someone can go further and warn peers that the individual may be adversely affected by short timescales. To get away from triggers, change the environment where possible, especially where the triggers are non-human entities. The bottom line is to ensure the mind is prepared and has little pressure when dealing with a challenging problem.

Learning to change thoughts is important. It may seem a simple strategy but most people are struggling to let go of their thoughts. Thoughts impact emotions, and subsequently emotional reactions, as indicated above. The persistence of current thoughts occurs because the mind attempts to solve pending problems, and sometimes this is useful. By using cognitive reappraisal one can substitute positive thinking for negative thoughts. Low self-esteem could also be related to adhering to negative thoughts.

Words that we use

You can't take back words, so when you're about to use abusive words in a fit of anger, be assured that they're going a long way to harm the person you're telling them. You might say that you don't mean them later, but the words have had their effect already. The use of hurtful words sometimes stems from a desire to make them feel the hurt you are feeling, but it's not necessary.

Positive/negative thoughts

Your emotions have a high influence on how you interpret different situations. You're more likely to view things with hope when you're happy, while depression causes anxiety and pessimism. Reflect on your emotional filter by reframing your thoughts, and take a more realistic approach.

When pessimism sets in, restructuring your thoughts involves embracing a more positive outlook. Not all situations have the same level of ease to present themselves. There's something, all you need to do is step back, look inward, separate your feelings, so you can have a strong line of thinking. The bottom line is to avoid ruminating on negatives when more is expected. You can easily lose control over how you handle the sensations. You should initiate tasks that will turn the brain's source of stress, such as taking a walk and doing a task.

CHAPTER 5

HOW NEGATIVE EMOTIONS AFFECT YOUR HEALTH

Our emotional distress often manifests as physical pain which causes negative changes in the body. If you've ever been so stressed out that you've found yourself over a toilet with your nose, or so angry that your vision starts going black and blotchy in the corners, then you understand how intense emotions can make us feel physically ill. You may have had chronic stomach pain for years, but because the cause is not physical but psychological, no doctor has been able to tell you why. It might be because it's the feelings that cause pain and not actual ailment.

Changes of appetite are a common physical symptom of poor emotional health. Many people who have depression experience a loss of appetite and a subsequent loss of weight. The body is still getting hungry because it needs nutrition to function, but even favorite foods can become flavourless and nasty. However, sugar affects the pleasure center of the brain, which is craving the good feelings caused by sugary foods. This could explain why depressed people sometimes gain weight and struggle with binge-eating.

The digestive problems are another common physical expression of intense negative emotion. The brain and the digestive tract are constantly communicating with each other, which is why you can get nauseous when anxious. If you undergo intense emotional pain it induces disturbance in your bowel's normal contractions. It also decreases immunity, making it easier for bacteria to penetrate the digestive tract.

You're Body on Anger

Anger is not always harmful, by itself. This points us to something or someone that is wrong with our life and motivates us to fix that and show our anger. Nevertheless, ceaseless anger and rage will affect your physical health.

Chronic or mismanaged stress and frustration can cause a variety of types of pain in the body and harm to personal health. A list of common physical symptoms triggered by negative stress and anger is given here:

- Accelerated heart rate
- Accelerated breathing rate
- Increased blood pressure

- General aches and pains
- Muscle tension and pain
- Jaw clenching/teeth grinding
- Stomach/digestive issues
- Lowered immune function
- Difficulty healing
- Dizziness and nausea
- Insomnia or trouble sleeping too much
- Loss of or increase in appetite
- Loss of sex drive
- Tinnitus/ringing in ears
- Eczema and other skin conditions

Stress and anger are not the only feelings that may experience physical pain. Depression can cause your physical health as much havoc as it can on your emotional health, causing a range of symptoms and worsening existing conditions. Most people experience the physical symptoms of depression but may not know that those symptoms have a psychological origin which makes it much more difficult to find solutions to these physical problems.

Impact of Negative Emotions on Health

Negative emotions have several other health implications, aside from the digestive problems. There are illnesses and health problems you've had in the past that you figured were caused by viruses but caused by overindulgence of radioactive fuels.

Heart Health

Negative emotions have the same sort of impact on the heart as pain. You tend to want to do a series of things when you're anxious, which will help you feel better. Some of these things may not be healthy for you because they include alcohol reliance, smoking, or over-eating comfort food.

Eating Disorders

When a person is struggling with negative emotions, the last thing on their mind is usually food. In that condition no feeding may or may not be deliberate. Yet fear also paves the way for eating disorders and this is true because in the past most people who are diagnosed with eating disorders suffer or may have experienced stress.

Feed conditions are illnesses. The people who experience them observe with eating a sudden change that is usually caused by their anxiety about weight gain and how they look.

Unplanned Weight Loss

You will be affected emotionally and physically by anything toxic; it will become apparent that you are going through something, and one of the physical manifestations is weight loss. Yes, we all want to keep a proper and healthy weight, but unplanned weight loss can be terrible, especially when you have eating disorders as well.

Your clothing won't fit properly any more. You will look exhausted and unsafe which will also cause more questions to be asked by people. Even if you weren't a very chubby person before this challenge, it would be too obvious to ignore the amount of weight that you shed.

Unplanned weight loss can also influence the mind of an individual, because if you don't understand the connection with your feelings and weight loss, you'll start thinking that you're very sick. Some people go to the doctor, hoping for a disease they don't have to be diagnosed for.

Toxic emotions have a way of getting you to put the source of your worry ahead of you; you don't take care of yourself anymore or put your wellbeing first. In most cases, some people realize that after a long time they had lost weight because their bodies were not being paid attention.

Unhealthy weight loss can make you vulnerable to fatigue and sickness. You'll still feel tired and with everything you do, this can lead to unproductivity. It's pretty amazing to think all of these health issues started with just one wrong idea. So does this mean we can use positive thinking to reverse the process?

How positive emotions affect your health

Everything else, even your health, feels excellent when you feel good. If you take the time to compare and contrast the state of your health when you feel anxious and when you are not, you would agree that when you are happy you feel healthier.

But aside from the "feeling" of being healthy, it's a fact that positive emotions have an excellent effect on mental and physical health — people who are happy fall ill less often than those who are anxious or depressed.

There is a new term known as "positive psychology" because of the impact of positive moods on health, which involves the use of various techniques that encourage us to identify and develop positive emotions for better health experiences.

Positive psychology emphasizes the fact that priority should be paid to problem-free feelings, while motivating people to rely more on their strengths and not on their shortcomings. Anxiety is often the product of the worst-case scenario uncertainty and concentrating yourself on the things you can't do while expecting disappointing results.

But you are encouraged to look beyond the anxiety that leads you to have eating and sleeping problems, using positive psychology. You are also empowered to construct the best things in your life and the worst to repair.

You need to thrive as an individual, and this also means you need to be in good health to achieve that, but good health is linked to your emotions, which brings us right back to the healing ability of good feelings.

If you have trouble sleeping because you are nervous, try to be happy and have less anxiety. You'll notice your sleep patterns are getting better. When you respect yourself above all and value your appearance, you wouldn't have problems with eating disorders or you'd be worried about your looks.

Being healthy isn't the absence of disease, and that's what positive psychology seeks to fully express. As well as being disease-free, your newfound optimism will help you enjoy good heart health. It will allow you to live a long and happy life where there is no burden on you to do anything but what you are.

We're not concerned about the immortality theory, which is all about how long we'll live. We are concerned about the impact and quality of life that we have and that is what matters. The good thing about this method of thought, though, is that while you're not necessarily focused on how long you're going to live, if you love positive emotions, you're guaranteed to have a long life in the cards.

What Takes Place in Your Brain When You Are All about Positive Emotions?

Negative emotions allow you to be completely committed to the source of your fear, which also makes it difficult for you to be fully aware of the other good things you've been doing for yourself. Unfortunately, the more you're narrow-minded about the issue, the more harm it does to your safety.

The stresses that you most commonly experience are because you find certain stuff very difficult and hard to manage, but when you have more positive emotions, it will make stressful situations easier to deal with. The thoughts you've identified as "hard" will become simple when positive emotions help you build resilience.

In another segment, we're going to talk more about emotional resilience but what you should know now is that positive emotions serve as a protection that prevents you from the struggles you may face with negative emotions.

Negative emotions keep you on reminding you of your problems. Talk about it: If you started to feel nervous, most of the time it was because you recalled something bad or you worried about a question that you would have to deal with later. However, this does not mean that when you focus on positive thoughts, you are indifferent to problems. Actually, this is not so!

Don't focus your attention too long on the issue, enough to get you angry, nervous or frightened. You'd think every day is horrible, with more emphasis on negative emotions. At the end of it, you will find you have nothing to be thankful for.

We begin to appreciate life more when we spend time thinking about the effect of positive emotions and what full reliance on it does for our health. We become open to more positive-driven conversations around.

You're Body on Positive Emotion

For as long as they have been researching the negative effects, psychologists have been studying the positive effects of feelings and it is usually found that people who feel more positive emotions tend to be healthier and live longer. When we feel more upbeat and positive, our bodies become better balanced, and our autonomic systems (especially the autonomous nervous system) function properly without the interference of stress hormones and other negative emotional physical consequences. If we consistently undergo positive interactions with others and ourselves, we supply our body with a period of stability and wellbeing.

CHAPTER 6

HOW TO CHANGE YOUR EMOTIONS

Assessing your emotional state is a key step in both honing your emotional intelligence and generally having empathy. Many individuals may be constantly taken care of in their emotional state, while others may go a day or a week without even worrying about it. While it can be tempting to fall into the trap of generalizations about the kind of people who think about their feelings and those who don't, the problem isn't as clear as it might seem.

Persons who report constantly talking about their feelings can be described as the sensitive, empathetic kind. These are the kinds of people that instinctively ask others how they feel, or who allow others to hear the news that indicates the other may be going through a time of trouble. Many people recognize their emotional state instinctively and this can cause them to be sensitive to other people's emotional states.

WHY DO EMOTIONS OFTEN TAKE CONTROL OF PEOPLE?

- **People don't Recognize Own Emotions as a Staging Ground**

Understanding your own emotions is the basis for understanding other people's emotions instead. That's why empathy and emotional intelligence doesn't consist of specific cognitive talents, but of many. This should lead people to realize that successful emotional intelligence involves tying together several emotional steps for the purpose of interconnectivity. If all you do is know your own feelings, then you don't grasp other people's emotions and therefore you don't respond with emotional intelligence.

Recognizing one's own feelings is therefore a starting point for action towards others with empathy. In fact, recognizing individual emotions alone does not lead directly within us to sympathy, empathy, or emotional intelligence. When men and women focus solely on understanding their own feelings but don't think about other people's emotions, instead they act with narcissism, which is the antithesis of the empathy this attempts to promote.

make yourself look better at that moment than any other person sitting in that room, and you don't have to pull that kind of shame on yourself. You met the president— nice. The brother of your father is the one on television— yes, that is cool. Not all need to know. Instead of making you look interesting, in want of attention, you come off as a braggart and this puts people off sincerely. Name dropping may make you feel better about yourself, but how do you think it's going to make others feel?

- **Subtle Bragging**

Subtle boasting, or modest boasting, is the act of bragging in a way that is not necessarily viewed as bragging. If you exercise gracious bragging, you don't know you're bragging, because you're just reserved by your own. This is something that we do between mates, innocently at times.

- **Screaming at People**

Nobody wants a screamer. No matter how much your screaming the person deserves, it isn't appropriate. If you yell at them you make people feel small and insignificant. Especially when yelling when you are angry at others is a regular habit of yours. They might tell that when you're angry, it's just your way of reacting and that screaming makes you feel much better but have you ever stopped caring how the other person feels about your screaming?

- **Gossiping**

If you whisper about someone else, it says more about you than about the other you were talking to. There is no use in basing the conversation on another's life; marriages that rely on speculation have a very shaky foundation and are likely to collapse sooner than later. Gossiping is an unhealthy habit, and it reflects a very low emotional intelligence state.

- **Talking a Lot More Than Listening**

It limits your chances of learning and of unlearning things when you speak more than you listen to. You're shoving your opinion down someone else's throat without giving them the time or opportunity to air theirs.

Sometimes listening helps you make a better choice. Never listening to people as they talk and being too concerned about expressing your own thoughts can make you look stupid. At some point, you're going to start saying things that don't make much sense, because you didn't listen first. You'll suddenly start looking ignorant, and no one wants to associate with an ignorant person who isn't willing to learn either.

- ## Posting Too Much of Yourself on Social Media

Such conduct is culpable to a lot of people. This reflects a need for recognition, and is generally expressed by the expression "putting everything out there." Ok, news flash, you don't have to do that. You don't really have to tell the world all the dreams you have after you wake up and before you go to bed, or all the things you do. The social media and those online don't need to verify you. They do not care about you so much. They shouldn't be aware of you so much. It is needless to throw these stuff into their faces. Save on to yourself some information. The internet has good memory, remember; it never forgets.

- ## Saying Too Much of Yourself Too Early in a Relationship

Not everyone has to know all the information that you sprinkle with them when you first speak to them. Too early sharing makes you get off as an attention seeker. This seems like you want the person to think you're genuine and transparent and almost instantly want them to like you. Letting the interaction flow organically is much easier, and then the rest of the details will come out spontaneously, without tension. It's also easier to relax when trying to build confidence in the relationship, and get to know the other person better. Too much exposure of yourself is rushing things and does not allow the other person a chance to be secure in the relationship.

- **Being Closed-Minded**

This is a daunting problem. It's important to look at things with an open mind. Keeping a closed mind renders you inaccessible. It also means that you already have a formed opinion about a certain thing, and you are unwilling to listen and make changes to your initial thoughts, making you inaccessible when approaching. Keeping an open mind is very sensible, and being open to change. These habits are associated with low-emotional intelligence people, and should be stopped now. They're harmful to you, the people around you, and your emotional intelligence is growing.

- **Avoidance**

Avoidance is similar to denial, but it is much more conscious. This occurs when we can deal with certain things, feelings or ideas by completely avoiding them. A person experiencing high levels of work stress, for example, can cease to show up for work. They minimize stressors in terms of removing the stress, but because we don't cope with the emotional trigger that creates more tension and more pain.

• Social Withdrawal

Most people who experience emotional turmoil will withdraw from friends and family. This is not to be confused with actually having to take some time alone, which we all sometimes need. If we feel too exhausted, overwhelmed or insecure about being around people whose company we once enjoyed, social withdrawal happens. Human beings desire contact, but isolation is easy to fall into, growing negative emotions such as depression and self-doubt.

• Compulsive Behavior

Compulsive behavior is the repeated engagement, usually to the point of obsession, in an activity despite the sense and reason. We engage in this type of behavior because it can provide temporary relief from negative emotions such as anxiety, stress, and grief, but it can exacerbate these problems by letting us feel out of control of our behaviors. Binge-eating, over-exercising, hoarding, cheating and pornography are forms of compulsive behavior. Such behaviors may seem very basic and trivial to those dealing with Obsessive-Compulsive Disorder, such as hand-washing, inspecting (doors, gas taps, light switches, etc.), ordering / organizing, and counting.

- **Self-Destructive Behavior**

Sometimes we find relief from negative emotions through temporarily pleasurable, but ultimately self-destructive, behaviors. Smoking cigarettes is a great example of self-destructive behavior, despite knowing this habit can cause health problems later in life. We are often aware of the negative consequences of such behavior, but for the relief it provides we engage in it anyway. Smoking, alcohol abuse, drug abuse, binge-eating and self-harm are common self-destructive behaviors.

CHANGE YOUR ENVIRONMENT TO CHANGE

Under that perspective, even though the feelings are identical, individuals respond to emotions in a customized way. When you feel upset, for example, the way you react to the emotion will be different from the way your colleague reacts. The consequence of responding personalized to every emotion is attributed to other emotional factors. The rates of resilience differ, for example, by person.

In addition, the environment also impacts on how we respond to emotions. Talk about how you respond in public to bad news, and when you're at home alone. Using a subjective view it is necessary to examine how one reacts to emotions.

In detail, different aspects of emotion are affecting how we respond to it. For example, the same emotion may have varying intensity. An example could be where you feel happy, but the degree of happiness in the crowd would differ per person. There is a chance that an individual who has enjoyed positive emotions for the whole week may not feel the happiness that others feel as intense. On the other hand, a person who has been depressed throughout the week may find the joy expressed as highly intense by others. In this situation the response to the emotion can vary because of the strength of the emotional feeling.

The subjective paradigm partially explains the complexity of the emotions, since each person processes each emotion uniquely despite the universal emotion. The subjective paradigms seem to assert that it is futile to focus on making each person react uniformly to emotion, and instead focus on generating the desired emotion rather than on how people will react to the emotion.

CHAPTER 7

OVERCOMING NEGATIVITY

It's important to build a positive mind state to get rid of all kinds of negativity from your life. It is only when you are conscious of your negative thoughts, fight them and consistently replacing them with constructive solutions that you prepare yourself to control and move past your extreme emotions. Here's how you can do this: If you catch yourself catastrophizing an instance's magnitude, reading too much into stuff, limiting someone who affects you to a two-dimensional mark, and making negative assumptions for something you don't feel too enthusiastic about, doubt the validity of those thoughts and emotions. For starters, if you see your friend losing interest in your conversation, and you jump straight to the conclusion that he / she has insulted you or does not want to be your friend anymore, hang on to that thought and challenge its genuineness. Ask yourself questions such as: Why am I feeling this way? What evidence do I need to validate my assumption? Has my friend behaved like that all along? What about all those times when he / she was compassionate toward me and listened patiently to my problems? These inquiries help you find evidence that makes it possible for you to determine the validity of your strong emotions and the negative thoughts they are stirring up. If you realize that because of your preconceived notions you are merely thinking negatively, you can easily distinguish between healthy and unhealthy feelings and can do away with the latter.

Also, whenever you think negatively of yourself or nurture a deep, negative belief in your capabilities, think of the emotion that stirred those thoughts and beliefs and question their authenticity. When you feel you can't win a prize, why do you think this is so? When you think it's because you're not working hard so you know exactly what you have to do to prove yourself wrong: work hard. To manage the negative thoughts and the underlying emotions that cause them, it is important to find out the root cause of a negative thought and then address it.

Once you're done analyzing a negative thought or belief, find and repeat a more realistic and positive substitute for it. For instance, if you thought,' I don't think I'll ever reach the break-even point in my business and struggle to improve sales forever,' turn it into something along the lines of,' my goal may be difficult, but it's possible-especially if I work hard to achieve it.' Such realistically positive thoughts make you feel hopeful and positive. Recall singing it repeatedly over and over again to immerse it in your subconscious mind. You activate the RAS (Reticular Activating System) as you continuously concentrate on something, which then perceives it as an essential piece of information, and sticks to it. Sometimes, you reinforce it to your subconscious mind, as you continually think about something. Once the subconscious is validated by something, it embraces it and gradually forms thoughts in that direction. Therefore, if you constantly feed your amygdala with constructive ideas, and talk about them day after day, you will quickly get rid of all negative thoughts and emotions and replace them with healthy and positive ones.

You can be happy, optimistic and successful in life and that can only happen if you choose to substitute negative thoughts with positive thoughts. If things don't go your way, it's natural to feel agitated, furious, and frustrated, but you need to teach yourself slowly not to hang on to those feelings, realize their consequences, and replace them with more optimistic ones by simply replacing ill thoughts with good. To learn to control your feelings, start working to conquer your negative thoughts and fears.

5 PROVEN STRATEGIES AND/OR THERAPIES TO ELIMINATE NEGATIVE EMOTIONS AND THOUGHTS

- **Develop self-awareness**

Self-awareness is about understanding yourself, being aware of what's going on in your life, and having an idea of how you see your daily life or job progressing. You need a certain degree of intelligence to be self-aware, and at least a vague sense of what you would like to do with your life. Once you know what you want, finding a method of getting it becomes easier. If you don't, you're left to drift aimlessly, with neither an objective nor a plan.

How can you develop awareness of yourself, then? Begin by increasing your sensitivity to your very own gut and emotions, as they are generally the closest friends you'll ever have to trust. Make an effort to set aside for self-reflection a while, and talk about your actions, feelings, desires, grievances, goals etc.

Many who are used to self-analyzing should probably find this straightforward, but if you're not used to this kind of analysis or this kind of thought, it may be challenging, even disturbing. Start by setting aside 30 minutes every night when you're done with the job for the day and can relax a little, and dream about the day or week behind you. If you particularly had a difficult day / week, ask yourself all you can find out from the experience.

This exercise has the function of really getting you used to knowing how you feel and why.

Or, you might start journalizing, and it's not about keeping a diary and covering your everyday thoughts and activities. Journaling is about capturing any unpleasant or odd events, feelings or emotions you may have had. Some things aren't easy to do with others, and anyway, it's not really all about blogging, so why not get it off your chest by writing it down. The great thing about journaling is generally that in order to write about something, you have to believe in what to write; in truth, it is often this method of learning about a question that lets you see what's at the heart. So if you feel upset, angry or disappointed write it down and move on.

- **Understand your emotions and what triggers them**

You have to be able to feel them to understand your feelings. It's sad how many people are afraid of their own emotions, especially negative ones, e.g. sadness, anger, bitterness, etc., and as soon as they feel these feelings take over, they perform something that can interrupt their thinking train, e.g. they can activate with something to distract themselves from these unpleasant emotions.

If you acknowledge yourself in this, you should know that all you will achieve in this way is to postpone (maybe indefinitely) facing your own demons and deal with whatever is troubling you. Feelings must be experienced and addressed, and not buried.

Intelligent people are not physically ashamed of their feelings. We stay at it for as long as it takes that the feeling end up being defined, whatever it really is we believe. There's a reason you feel like you're doing, and instead of ignoring them, you should try to "decipher" your emotions because they try to let you know.

You first have to be able to understand yourself to become competent at learning others. And, the feelings you really don't want to feel should be confronted, assessed and let go.

• **Listen without judging**

Good listeners are uncommon, mostly because it involves a lot of patience, willingness to give up your time and attention for others, and mental energy while you listen.

A strong listener's main trait is to pay attention with empathy, and that means without judgment. This is not always straightforward, and may be complicated in a few complete situations, so if you realize that you're biased towards someone, perhaps it's best not to talk to them if you think that you've already made up your mind about how you feel about what they're going to say.

Therefore, you will try and be attentive during the talk to become a great listener, and stay focused. This can be complicated as some other people don't stop talking or have a difficulty explaining what they say so you might be looking at a couple of hours. But if you're not really interested in this person, or you're in a rush, or you're not feeling well, then try to postpone the conversation for another time. The tell-tale indicators of disinterest or indifference, such as staring at your watch or checking your mobile phones or computer, can be extremely insulting and disrespectful to the person you're talking to.

Those who are emotionally intelligent display concern in others by allowing them to talk even more (even if they don't agree with what they're saying), and by having a forum where it's safe to start to say something you think.

And, the next time you talk to someone who wants your input, support or just a shoulder to cry on, try to be compassionate (some people have a long time to get to the point), concentrated (reserve this time confined to them and shut off your phone), and non-judgmental (provide them with the benefit of a doubt). Not only can you help the person by not becoming and judging open-minded by giving them the opportunity to get something off their upper body, but you can also gain insight into what's going on in your team, or a family.

Focus also on your and their body language, e.g. voice modulation, facial expression, body posture, etc. To a casual observer, these are obvious signs of how both of you feel about the conversation.

Active listening takes a lot of practice, but it's one of the things you should do every day, where you're unaware of, and what you really listen to.

• **Mind-Body Connection**

This is about listening to your body and knowing what they are trying to tell you. According to the theory of the mind-body relation, discomfort in a part of your body is certainly a good indicator that something is wrong. Lower back discomfort, for example, is linked to financial problems, upper back discomfort to being overwhelmed by life, a tummy knot with nervousness or fear etc.

Learning how to identify and perceive these signs will help you save much time and trouble in learning why you are feeling a certain way.

But, what often happens is that while your body tells you that you're anxious, anxious, angry or harmful, you simply ignore these symptoms, hoping that they will eventually go away.

Unfortunately, Western culture pays an excessive amount of importance to feel happy and high at all times, so folks are not encouraged to deal with their negative feelings, but are advised to ignore them, e.g. by repeating positive affirmations, or repairing them, by taking something that will make them experience better. Do you really think that you will finally become healthy, optimistic and courageous if you forget your negative emotions, do it a mantra again or take something to make you feel high??

Often, when you're overcome by feelings, it may be safe to quiet yourself straight down, even in unhealthy ways, until you can think clearly. However, this gives only temporary respite and is not a solution to your problem.

Emotional intelligence can help you get under your feelings by teaching you how to work out exactly what the causes are, and how to perceive and unleash those emotions in the least harmful fashion.

- **Engage**

How do you become involved with your community? Are you volunteering? Is there someone who you deal out regularly, emotionally or otherwise by moral support? Are you there for others if they need you, even though you know it is going to spoil your weekend with your family that you wanted to spend in?

Empathy is the primary trait of emotionally intelligent people, and anyone can easily develop it if they follow a few simple tips on how to develop or improve these abilities. Yet, by doing it, the best way to develop empathy may be. Simply put, you do what emotionally intelligent people do whenever you engage with others: you listen, you try to understand and you listen in.

Nevertheless, because of the fact that they would like to be studied solely because they are emotionally intelligent, often people show empathy. They say the right thing, are always politically correct, seem to be filled with deep empathy, listen carefully, offer help etc. But, if they're caught off-safeguard or if they don't feel in the mood for putting up an act for a few good reasons, their true character comes out easily. Today, if you see yourself as a head in particular, to advance professionally, you have to prove that you have a high psychological intelligence, so usually those who fake it do that for self-promotion.

The best way to improve your sensitivity is to begin taking interest in others, such as how they work, what disturbs them, how they deal with it, etc. Develop your listening skills and seek to have at least one conversation in depth every month. You'll automatically increase your emotional intelligence when communicating with others.

- **Develop self-management**

Self-management is about controlling your emotions, not feeling you're suppressing them or ignoring them, but figuring out how to handle them and releasing them only after you've processed and understood them. It's also about self-management being true to you. Some of the real ways you can improve your self-administration are by developing your integrity, e.g.:

- Practice what you preach
- Be prepared to speak out, even if you risk being made fun of
- Do not make promises that you are unlikely to keep
- Continually be polite and respectful with your colleagues, it doesn't matter how close you may be
- Be self-disciplined, especially if you anticipate that of others.

131

- **Learn to cope with criticism**

Negative feedback is usually undeserved and is not fully aware of your performance as a result of the person presenting it, or perhaps using the opportunity to sabotage your self-confidence, or openly undermine your job.

However, if truth is told, there is usually a grain of truth in Atlanta divorce lawyers who give negative feedback. Though there may have been very good reasons why you've been underperforming or experiencing a score of people complaining about you, the truth is that you have failed. Nevertheless, when you arrive at a point where you can embrace negative opinions or open criticism without accepting it, you prove that you have personal self-confidence as well as relational maturity.

So, how can we get more open to negative feedback? First of all, not all critiques are equally important, nor should you react to them in the same way. The comment of a friend about your brand-new hairstyle is actually a sign that she's making fun of you, but it may be a subtle suggestion that you don't like the look.

Besides, if you receive less than satisfactory feedback repeatedly on your own performance, or behavior, instead of sulking or throwing a tantrum, try to look inside yourself through the eyes

Remember how you feel as you breathe in and breathe out, your mouth, neck, lungs and abdomen. Concentrate on air flow in and out of your abdominal cavity. Having just a few deep breaths will make you feel better and while communicating with others you will be in a positive frame of mind.

Each time you find yourself diverting focus away from your breath, acknowledge the sensation softly without punishing it and transfer the focus back into your body. Live consciously in the present moment. Stop thinking about the past or the future, and just concentrate on breathing. Your frequency of the emotions will change in no time.

Practice mindfulness in all spheres of life (focusing attention on the present moment in a purposeful and non-judgmental manner) to relax your spirit (especially if you happen to be a more hot-tempered or easily irritable individual).

Through learning in a non-judgmental way to examine your emotions and feelings, you not only increase your understanding of these feelings with greater clarity but also reduce your chances of being overcome by a bunch of negative or damaging emotions.

- **Question Your Perspective**

The first step to enhancing your emotional intelligence and social skills is to recognize multiple ways of looking at a situation. Even though you may think your perspective or way of looking at things is right, get into the habit of looking at it from different angles rather than giving in to knee-jerk reactions.

If you're angry or upset with someone, stop impulsive reactions. Alternatively, slow down, and consider different ways to explain the circumstances. What are the different explanations for the situation? You can, of course, still stick to your viewpoint but at least try to look at it from different angles before approaching the situation more calmly and rationally. At best, even if you don't change your perspective on the situation, you'll have more time to calm down and think about a more positive, constructive response.

- **Celebrate Positive Emotions to Attract More of Them**

Emotionally smart people who experience more positive energy lead to more fulfilling relationships and are more resilient in responding to negative situations. So get into the habit of doing things intentionally that induce a sense of happiness and happiness within you.

There are several ways to bring more love to your soul by committing random acts of kindness, expressing gratitude, being in the middle of nature, walking, participating in enjoyable activities, creative visualization and remembering past experiences that have given you pleasure. Celebrating positive emotions helps generate more of this positive attitude, which helps to create positive experiences.

- **Know Yourself like No One Else**

The epicenter of emotional intelligence knows that no-one else likes you. Self-awareness is the secret to achieving a greater intelligence of the emotions. Having a good understanding of your core features, qualities, shortcomings, interests, principles, behaviors and other related facets of your personality helps you understand your positive and negative causes.

When you gain complete self-awareness, you will understand what drives your responses and how you can manage them more effectively. By personality tests, meditation, input from others and more, an individual may gain greater self-awareness.

Try to relate the feelings to the actions or activities arising from those emotions. Who powers the impulse? -individual feelings would spur you to behave the way you do?

CHAPTER 8

HOW TO READ EMOTIONS

By understanding how emotions associate with the many aspects of emotional intelligence, we can approach the subject in a healthy manner. Some of the stigmas that come from so-called emotional people are that people who are labeled as emotional may not engage in the related steps of understanding the emotions, self-regulation and empathy of other people. This has been touched upon in the topic of narcissism, but those who accept their emotions healthily often tolerate others ' emotions and know how to control their emotions should they tend to interfere with social interactions.

That perception has to do with the idea that thinking too much about emotions is a negative thing. Such distorted beliefs caused some people to hide in any feeling while others took the opposite path and became proponents of moral and rational reasoning. But in the case of emotion, this is a downward spiral that results from not using terminology appropriately. Showing compassion for someone is an indication you are feeling anxious. Emotional feeling infuses all religions and people become better friends, better family members and better lovers because they care.

Emotion is the groundwork for meaningful social relations. Having emotions doesn't mean you're pinched by them, which is how some people characterize the term. Through denying emotion or mischaracterizing emotion, we create a society where individuals either have skewed feelings because they don't perceive them properly or they don't feel emotion at all because they've been conditioned to be wary about emotion based on myths.

Coping with negative feelings is never easy and simple. By listening to the body you can start identifying your repressed emotions. The body is often as affected as the mind when dealing with repressed emotions, especially the anger and rage. Repressed rage can cause chronic pain as well as other mental upheavals such as high anxiety and depression.

Total fitness is not just about mental and emotional health; it's also about physical health. There isn't separately your physical and psychological selves exist. They communicate with each other on a permanent basis. Hold on reading to find out how your poor emotional health can negatively affect your body and physical well-being.

Knowing how our minds function is one of the greatest mysteries we have yet to solve. A lot of people have devoted their entire lives to knowing the mind, unfortunately to no avail. Understanding the roles of our mind and emotion toward our well-being is of paramount importance as it puts us in the driving seat to control our lives. This is just a small part of our quest to use the mind to control our thoughts, but it should not be overlooked. Ignoring the interactions between our minds, emotions, thoughts and feelings means we will ignore their roles, similar to the relationship held by every part of our entire make-up. On a more serious note, this could be an aspect we need to fix before taking any further steps.

Mind and body don't operate independently. We are not separate systems, and when we are tensed, that can be seen. An instance of a nervous moment is a job interview, or a first date with our long-term crush. No matter how calm and confident we would like to look in such instances; we find that at the same time we are both tensed and self-conscious. As a result of the self-conscious sensation we are having, the muscles in our buttocks will be stretched. We sweat more than normal, and in such cases we may even feel nauseous, not forgetting those moments where we need or seek to be sure we can fluff our sheets.

Our feelings which are created by the subconscious and highly influenced by our mind's unconscious layer are what add value to our thinking. Let us presume you've been raised to believe, for example, that flipping a salt shaker over is a sign of bad luck. If you watch someone unintentionally tipping a salt shaker, or you do so, your mind sends out thoughts that project emotions.

Our sensations are expressions of our state of existence, both emotional and mental. Typically linked to our tactile physical and social emotions, they're used to respond to happiness, anxiety, affection, anger, sorrow, hatred, enjoyment, and a host of other feelings. We must regulate and manipulate certain emotions and feelings in other ways to prevent harmful actions that usually come at high cost.

Managing your feelings can be compared to creating an ability. It implies learning how to do something better. In our side, that needs improvement. In reality we are struggling as humans to accept change. This is largely due to many factors, but in this regard the workings of the mind are highly influential as we discussed part of this book earlier. Controlling your emotions will make you feel stronger mentally. The good thing is, it can all profit from managing their emotions. Here's why you should keep an eye on your feelings.

Keeping your feelings in check is not the same as managing those feelings. Ignoring how you felt about some case isn't going to make the emotions go anywhere. Rather, such feelings will get worse if they aren't addressed with time properly.

- **Create a Room in Your Life for Joy**

Just mindful of what positivity can do is not enough for you. You have to be intentional about it by creating space for the right activities to help you attain great emotions. People often ask how they can create happiness in their lives, and I must agree that communicating with the right people is one way of doing that.

If in a circle of friends there are positive and happy people, the joy will be contagious, so even if one person feels the smallest form of anxiety, it will be cut off immediately. That when you connect with positive vibes from the right people, your mental health gets a boost.

Being around positive people doesn't mean your problems fly off the window, and it's sunshine and rainbows all over again. It only means you know there are issues but you enjoy yourself too much to take your happiness from the problems.

You have to have all your goals listed. What do you think is most important? Health? Wealth? Look out for anything that matters most to you. If you're all about getting good health, you need to be deliberate about being surrounded by the right people while investing in emotional interactions of quality.

Meditation is an essential tool for keeping you connected to positive emotions. Speak of negative emotions as much chaos that has no sense but separates you from your mental and physical well-being. On the other hand, positive thoughts flourish in meditative sessions where the mind is at ease, and you don't get overwhelmed by negative emotions.

Your ability to take control of your emotions will determine the type of interactions that you have with your wellbeing and the good feelings that it generates within you.

• Listen to Your Body

If your body is trying to say something to you, don't ignore it. It may be too easy to attribute physical discomfort to normal changes in the body, such as ageing, when your physical symptoms may actually be caused by your emotional turmoil. It is also important to note that pre-existing illnesses for no clinically apparent cause deteriorate. When we cope with other diseases, chronic stress and anxiety can damage our bodies.

• Connect with Others

The professionals studying the physical impact of negative emotions found that there is a direct connection between perceived positive connections and improved physical health with others. The more good social interactions we have, the better we are at manifesting positive emotions within ourselves, and vice-versa, which relieves a lot of physical stress to the body. If we are able to maintain this' upward curve cycle' between positive emotion and positive social interaction, we will be able to grow more comfortably in our inner selves and thereby enhance our wellbeing.

- **Practice Relaxation**

Another great way of counteracting the negative physical effects of intense negative emotion is through calming exercise. Once we consciously relax, it helps to shut off or restart all the natural processes that can cause harm within the body (such as combat-or-flight), providing relief from stress hormones, muscle tension, and other physical symptoms. The meditation practice is an important and beneficial form of calming therapy.

- **Analyze Your Response**

Take the time to analyze these when you turn to face your negative emotions. Ask yourself, "Is the scale of the situation appropriate to this reaction? Is this emotional response anything to tell me? What can I do to change the situation? How can I benefit from this situation to better respond to future situations? To this step it's very important to use your practice of mindfulness. By getting to know our emotional selves better we can understand our emotional responses better and change them better.

- **Practice Breath Control**

If you feel an intense negative emotion such as anxiety, fear or rage, take a deep breath and try to take steady, regulated breath while concentrating your mind on the air. This act may help lower blood pressure and slow a high heart rate. If you have trouble focusing you can count the number of breaths you take. Breath awareness is an important part of many stress relief activities, including yoga, tai chi, and meditation.

- **Letting go of your emotions**

Emotions are energy in motion, but what happens if you do not want the energy to move? It's piling up. Through repressing your feelings, you are interrupting the normal flow of energy.

Unfortunately, no one has taught you how to handle your emotions or even that both positive and negative emotions are a natural phenomenon. Instead, they told you that you should suppress your negative emotions because they are bad.

You may have repressed the feelings for years, as a result. You encourage them to sink deeper into your subconscious by doing so, allowing them to become part of your identity. Often they have been phenomena you might not be sure of. Perhaps, for starters, you believe you're not good enough. Or maybe you regularly experience guilt. These are the results of the core beliefs that you developed through repression of your emotions over time.

Most of us have excessive emotional baggage and need to learn to let go. We need to declutter our minds to rid ourselves of the negative emotions that prevent us from living life to the fullest.

How to Condition Your Mind for Better Emotions

One effective way of conditioning the mind for better emotions is by managing impulses. Most of the emotions express themselves in an impulsive form. Allowing emotion to express itself fully always seems fulfilling as it allows the emotional energy to be restored within a short time. The author argues the best approach to conditioning the mind to realize better emotions is to handle impulses.

- **Managing Impulses**

The instinct applies to an unexpected, rapid feeling. An impulse is an impelling urge or emotion. Handling an impulse will require purposeful attempts to increase or depress the emotional intensity, including committing not to act upon a desire. The vital skills to manage an emotion include decision-making and awareness of where you center energy. Remember that our feelings emanate from our minds and this statement means that understanding how to control our thoughts can lead to better emotional regulation. Learn to focus or separate yourself from individual thoughts as an anger management strategy. It can be argued that how to make a decision and control where the mind is drawn to will lead to improved impulses management.

One should learn to stop the urge to act upon a desire accordingly. You should develop emotional awareness, including social awareness, which is arguably true. There are several ways to achieve impulse control, and one way is to develop emotional sensitivity by keeping a journal of your feelings and how you react to it. By having a journal of frequent emotions and how they express themselves, an intervention can be developed that attempts to stop the trigger factors that spur that emotion. For example, if on certain days you feel irritated and you can determine the underlying causes, then it is best to manage those

to the small initial favor, making the user more willing to cooperate with the larger offer.

A friend, for example, wants you to have her two children babysit for an hour or two. He then asks if you can just babysit the children for the remainder of the day, until you consent to the smaller offer.

Since you have already agreed to the smaller request, you might feel obliged to consent to the bigger request as well. This is a great example of what psychologists call the interaction theory, and advertisers often use it tactic to persuade consumers to purchase products and services.

- **Go Big and Then Small**

The foot-in - the-door approach is the reverse of that approach. A salesperson may start by making an unreasonable, sometimes broad request. The person reacts by refusing, slamming the door figuratively on the deal.

The salesperson responds by making a much smaller offer, which often turned out to be conciliatory. People frequently feel obliged to answer these offers. Because they rejected the initial request, people still feel compelled into approving the smaller request, to support the salesperson.

HOW TO INCREASE WILLPOWER

1. Feed our brains with regular, protein rich meals

Don't miss out on meals. The brain is the muscle decision making and its capacity to provide us with the required energy to make the right choices is determined by whether it is fed properly.

Therefore, we will eat regular meals, preferably low-glycemic foods, nutritious proteins, veggies and complex carbohydrates, so we can avoid the rush of glucose (associated with sugar and simple carbs) that inevitably plummet.

2. Keep it simple: work on one change at a time

Willpower can be increased but it is a slow and gradual cycle (just as muscle mass is increasing). And we work with a fixed amount of it on a daily basis (though that amount will change with experience over time).

We cannot change everything at once and at stressful times we can not radically change our lives. If we want real change we will start small and approach one long-term goal at a time.

3. Take a bite of dark chocolate for a quick energy boost

We are sometimes in a place where we have to make a quick decision and it feels difficult. We should be enjoying a taste of dark chocolate. Definitely bad. The small boost of strength will help our brains make choices.

Clearly, eating healthy, slow burning foods is much easier to provide our brains with a constant source of fuel, but in the event of an emergency "will-power," indulging a little is not a bad thing. Indeed it will help to increase our willpower.

4. Get a good night's sleep

Adequate rest increases our self-control and allows the brain an optimal environment for working. Rest reduces the need for glucose in the blood, which helps the body to take better advantage of what we have. For an adult, sufficient rest is typically 7-8 hours a night, and for a child, 10-12 hours a night.

Self-control needs brain power and our bodies usually don't provide enough glucose to our brains when we're exhausted.

5. Steer clear of temptation

People with lots of self-control don't have to use their discipline as often as they do. Hence it is high and in steady supply when willpower is needed.

So we can raise our willpower by not placing ourselves in positions where willpower is needed-steering out of those "danger spots" where pressure is present and willpower is needed.

HOW TO STOP PROCRASTINATING

- **Recognize That You're Procrastinating**

You may be putting off a job because you had to manage the workload again. Unless, for a genuinely good cause, you are shortly delaying an important task, then you are not actually procrastinating. When you start putting something off forever, though, or switching attention because you want to postpone doing something, so you certainly can.

- **Work out why you're procrastinating**

Before you can start tackling it, you need to understand the reasons why you procrastinate.

Would you dislike a particular task for example, if you find it boring or unpleasant? If so, take steps to easily get it out of the way, so you can concentrate on the parts of your work you find most rewarding.

Weak management may result in tardiness. It is easily solved by organized people because they use goal lists to create effective plans. Such methods help you arrange your activities according to goals and time limits.

And if you're coordinated, a mission can still make you feel exhausted. Maybe you have concerns about your abilities and are concerned about disappointment, so you're putting it off and seeking comfort in the work you know you're qualified to do.

Many people worry about success as much as about disappointment. We claim success would lead them to get swamped by demands to take on more roles.

Perfectionists are astonishingly frequently procrastinators. Also, instead of doing it imperfectly, they would rather stop doing a job that they do not believe they have the abilities to be doing.

Poor decision-making is another big cause of procrastination. When you can't decide what to do, in case you do the wrong thing, you'll probably put off taking action.

- **Adopt Anti-Procrastination Strategies**

Procrastination is a phenomenon-a behavior pattern that is deeply ingrained. This means you can't really crack it immediately. Behaviors just stop being behaviors if you quit doing them, so use as many approaches as possible below to give you the best chance to succeed.

  - Pardon yourself in the past for procrastinating. Studies show that self-forgiveness will help you feel more optimistic about yourself and diminish the risk of potential procrastination.

- Devise the plan. Concentrate on, not stop. Write down the things you need to do, and assign a time to complete them. That will motivate you to approach your job proactively.

- Offer a recognition for yourself. If you're completing a challenging task on time, reward yourself with a treat like a slice of cake or a cup from your favorite coffee shop. Just make sure you remember how well doing stuff sounds!

- Demand that someone test you out. Pressure on colleagues works! That's the idea behind social self-help. If you don't have someone to question, an online tool like Procraster will help you control yourself.

- Do as you go. Tackle the tasks as soon as they emerge, instead of allowing them to build up over another day.

- Rephrase the internal dialogue. Of example, the words "requires" and "shoulds" suggest that you have no say in what you do. This can make you feel disenfranchised and even lead to self-sabotage. Saying, "I choose to," though, means you own a job, and you can feel more in control of your workload.

- Rising disruptions. Switch off your email and social media while you're running, and avoid sitting somewhere near a TV!
- First thing, every day, try to "kill an elephant beetle!" Get those things you find least fun out of the way early on. That will allow you the remainder of the day to focus on the work you find most fun.

CHAPTER 9

HOW TO USE YOUR EMOTION TO GROW

Emotions and Finances

On the positive side some emotions can make taking risks easier for one. People who can process negative emotions and exhibit moderate positive emotions may, for example, take risks and invest in the stock market. To take risks one has to be prepared psychologically for both positive and negative results. In other words, one has to display the ability to deal with negative emotions and recover in good time. Those with a positive outlook are likely to take risks even if the economy fails to deliver on goals. If you feel energized, confident, and hopeful, then it's not a big deal to take a risk and invest. Marketers understand this and are going to invest time in getting the right feelings before they allow you to buy their product.

Emotions and Love

Positive emotions can make you more lovable. Showing positive emotions makes one easily relatable in almost all situations and that makes the person more lovable. Try to think about your school days or jobs, and see which people you want. Positive emotions will draw more people to you. There's a high likelihood that you prefer a person who shows happiness, hope, and motivates himself over a gloomy person. Since feelings can be contagious, the positive emotions can inspire the other person to feel positive. Although positive emotions are beneficial, bottling up negative emotions in an attempt to win respect and affection is counter-productive. Every emotion is necessary, and should be expressed.

Emotions and Personal Success

Managed feelings can improve personal success, whether positive or negative. Personal success in this context means positive social interactions, social relationships and better financial performance. On the positive side, feelings positively affect relationships and the handling of personal life, which improve personal success. Think of a person who is inspired, content and resilient. The individual is also likely to respond well to others.

Emotions and relationships

For emphasis, enhancing your emotion can help when you need to be assertive in relation management. There are a lot of misunderstandings about assertiveness as some people think it portrays one as being strong, arrogant or static. Assertiveness is important since it helps to express your limits and position. Assertiveness does not mean that they do not listen to others or are inflexible. In this way, assertiveness in a relationship can be a source of friction when the idea of assertiveness is not recognized by one or both of the parties. One example is where an entity attempts to express his or her viewpoint and the other party misconstructs that to suggest the opinion of the former has to prevail at the detriment of others. Nonetheless, one can interpret the other person's emotions with emotional intelligence, and take into account when expressing personal views.

In fact, raising your feelings would definitely promote effective settlement of disputes with others. Due to the unique nature of human behavior, conflicts are unavoidable in life and especially at the workplace. Many contemporary places of work are complex, which increases the risk of confrontation. Various places of work may see conflicts arising from other workers ' cultural insensitivity, gender stereotypes, race, religion, and socioeconomic aspects. All of these contribute to making a depriving sight of a workplace. If each employee can recognize their emotions, it becomes easier to make others aware of how they feel and this can facilitate conflict prevention.

BENEFITS OF BOOSTING SELF CONFIDENCE

- Improved sense of self-worth-the more self-confidence an individual has, the greater their self-esteem and skills. And this is what produces the sensation in life of "holding your head up high!"
- More fun and happiness in life-the more relaxed you are, the happy you are with yourself and the more you love what life has to offer. It is so easy!
- Less uncertainty and anxiety-You can embrace, adjust, understand, improve and benefit from any situation in life when confidence is high. This way, you automatically substitute fear and anxiety with greater self-confidence and ability.
- Protection from social anxiety-the more confident you are in your self-worth, the less concerned you are about what others think of you in social situations-this helps you to enjoy people more easily.
- Greater peace of mind and less pain-liberation from self-doubt, fear and anxiety inevitably transforms into greater peace of mind and a more stress-free life.
- The desire and drive to act-the more assured you are that you can achieve things you want to do (such as personal goals or dreams), the more inspired and driven you are to take action to achieve them!

- More achievement—if it was ever a puzzle that people who are self-confident seem to be more successful, now you know! Each of the above advantages will help you accomplish things you want to do faster and easier, ensuring you'll find more success in life.

HOW TO CONTROL LIGHT EMOTIONS

1. Bright light can heighten emotions.

Under brighter lighting we could feel both positive and negative emotions more intensely. In a 2014 survey, researchers asked volunteers to determine a hypothetical person's aggressiveness, three women's beauty, and various spicy chicken wing sauces appealing to them. They have asked volunteers to talk about a series of optimistic, negative, and neutral terms they thought. Generally, volunteers in a brightly illuminated room found the character more violent and the women more desirable than those in a dimly lit room. We also expressed a preference for spicier chicken wing sauces and used the positive and negative terms more intensely. When it came to both negative and positive feelings participant responses under brighter lights were more intense.

2. Blue light can make us feel more energetic

During the day, exposure to blue light will give us some extra energy and alarm us even more. A recent study found that subjects exposed to short wavelength, high energy blue light were more productive: they were able to accomplish cognitive tasks faster and more accurately than a group of controls. Blue light not only improved their alertness during exposure but also for a full half hour after exposure to blue light stopped.

3. It can become a problem at bedtime

Although blue light can give us a much-needed energy boost during the day, it can also make nighttime sleep more difficult for us. In the hours before bedtime, exposure to blue light from smartphones and tablets suppresses the development of the sleep-inducing hormone melatonin throughout our bodies, which can make it difficult for us to drift off to sleep. As you've probably noticed if you've ever tried to sleep at night, sleep deprivation has a whole host of mental and physiological side effects, ranging from impaired judgment and increased blood pressure to higher. So while blue light can provide a good morning pick-me-up, you may want to shut off your laptop only a couple hours before bedtime.

4. Natural light could make you happier

Catching a few normal midday rays of sunshine will make a world of difference. One research in 2014 found that people who had windows in their workplace exercised more, slept longer (on average, 46 minutes more than a night!), and had a greater sense of well-being overall than those whose offices had no windows. Researchers believe that natural light sensitivity allows our bodies to adhere to their normal circadian rhythms, and they know when to feel alert and active, and when to feel sleepy.

5. It may help reduce symptoms of depression.

Natural light may even help to reduce depressive symptoms. For one study for 2013, researchers found that seven weeks of improved sunlight exposure (in the form of increased outdoor time) appeared to reduce depressive symptoms for individuals with both vitamin D deficiency and depression. Those results were corroborated by another report in 2015. Instead of spending more time outdoors, the 2015 study involved volunteers in light therapy, a process that involves daily, prolonged exposure to lamps designed to simulate natural outdoor light. Researchers found that a combination of light therapy and antidepressants are significantly more effective than anti-depressants alone in treating depression. Daylight alone, of course, cannot cure depression— but researchers believe that natural light can be a useful tool for alleviating the symptoms.

CONCLUSION

Emotions are primarily found in the unconscious meaning we have far less control over how feelings emerge. That's why body language is important when deciding an individual's true status as the unconscious affects much of the vocabulary of the body. The feelings are strongly controlled with all those changes. The book constantly stressed that the emphasis should not be on suppressing feelings but on encouraging them to occur in a safe manner. Many people are wrongly thinking that negative emotions should not be communicated ignoring that emotions are a form of energy, and they need to dissipate.

While reading the book, we hope you'll understand why those with higher emotional intelligence have a better chance of being professionally successful and feeling more emotionally accomplished.

Your path to success depends on a lot of things, but mostly how well you continue to maneuver through your life. Developing emotional intelligence will help keep you on board.

In your life you will continue to experience negative emotions, but hopefully any time you realize that your emotions are not you and you will learn to accept them as they are before you let them go. You're not sad, upset, jealous, or angry; you're the object of those thoughts. After these fleeting emotions fade away you are what remains.

You're here to control the feelings. Know from them as much as you can, and then let them go. Do not cling to them as if you rely on them for your life. It just isn't. Don't associate with them, as if they were describing you. They don't. You are beyond feelings instead using the emotions to develop and recall.

MASTER YOUR THINKING

The Ultimate Guide to Empath Healing and to Stop Negative Thinking. Improve Your Emotional Intelligence with Self Esteem. Master Your Emotions and Improve Decision Making

By Jon Power

Summary

INTRODUCTION

You are an absolutely good person. You deserve a beautiful life, full of achievement, joy, happiness and enthusiasm. You have the right to have happy relationships, excellent health, meaningful work and freedom from capital. These are your birthright. That is what is supposed to happen in your life.

You are built to excel and have high levels of self-esteem, self-respect and personal pride. You are extraordinary; in all of mankind's history on earth, there has never been someone just like you. You have absolutely amazing untapped talents and abilities which can get you everything you might ever want in life when fully released and implemented.

You live in the greatest moment of all human history. You are surrounded by plenty of opportunities to make the most of and fulfill your goals. The only true limits on what you can, do, or have are the limitations that your own perception imposes upon yourself. Your future is practically boundless.

How did you react to the three paragraphs? You probably got two reactions. First of all, you loved what they said and your dearest wish was that they were valid for you. Yet, possibly, your second answer was one of cynicism and denial. Even though you sincerely wish to lead a perfectly safe, happy, prosperous life, your worries and fears emerged instantly as you read those words to remind you why these hopes and aspirations might not be possible for you.

Perhaps the most important mental and spiritual concept ever learned is that most of the time you become what you believe. The outside universe is a mirror image of your inner world. What's happening outside of you is a snapshot of what's going on inside. You can tell a person's inner state by looking at his or her life's outer circumstances. And it can't be any other way.

Your mind is incredibly powerful. Your emotions influence almost everything that happens to you, and decide everything. You can raise or lower your heart rate, boost or interfere with your metabolism, change your blood's chemical composition and help you sleep or stay awake at night.

You will make your feelings happy or sad, sometimes in a moment. You will warn you and make you conscious, or tired and distressed. They will make you popular or infamous, positive or negative, comfortable or nervous. You may feel powerful or weak in your mind, a survivor or a victor, a hero or a coward.

Your thoughts will make you a winner or a disappointment in your material life, wealthy or poverty-stricken, valued or forgotten. Your emotions, and the actions they cause, form your entire life. And the best news of all is they're totally under your own guidance.

You are a dynamic package of emotions, feelings, behaviors, expectations, pictures, worries, aspirations, concerns, beliefs and goals, often changing constantly, sometimes from second to second. Each of these factors influences the others in your temperament, sometimes in unpredictable ways. The whole of your life is the product of these variables intertwining and interconnecting.

The words and photos activate the feelings, and the emotions that go with them. Such images and feelings are causing actions and attitudes. Then your actions have consequences and outcomes which decide what's happening to you.

When you think about performance and confidence, you're going to feel confident and comfortable and you're going to perform well at whatever you do. If you're thinking about making mistakes or being humiliated you're going to perform badly, no matter how good you are.

From your imagination or from the external influences, pictures and photographs generate thoughts, feelings and actions that relate to them. We then cause acts that yield those consequences and tests. A person's thinking or circumstance can immediately cause you to feel happy or sad, elated or furious, caring or lonely.

Positive or negative, constructive or destructive, your behaviors contribute to the resulting images, feelings and actions that affect your life and relations. In turn, your behaviors are based on your previous experiences, and your simple assumptions on how life should be.

The feelings and perceptions that come with them are caused by your actions. You should actually act your way into emotion in a manner consistent with the conduct, by the Law of Reversibility. Through behaving as if you're always healthy, positive and confident, you'll soon start feeling that way inside. So your behaviors are completely under your influence, although your feelings are not.

The exterior dimensions of your life are good, in and of themselves. Only the sense you offer them defines your beliefs, thoughts, feelings and reactions to them. When you change your perspective about any part of your life, the way you feel and respond in that area will change. And since you can only decide what to do, you have the capacity to take complete control of your life.

The Law of Attraction states you are a "moving magnet" and inevitably draw the people, ideas, incentives and situations in accordance with your prevailing thoughts into your life.

If you think about hopeful, happy, caring and productive feelings, you generate a magnetism force field that draws the very things you're talking about, like iron filings to a magnet. This rule explains that it is you don't have to think about where the success can come from. If you can keep your mind clearly focused on what you want and refrain from worrying about what you don't want, just when you're ready you'll receive everything you need to achieve your goals. Shift your feelings, and change your life.

Successful people are the ones who think more creatively than people who have failed. We have different approaches to their lives, relationships, aspirations, challenges and experiences than others. We sow better plants, and we reap happier lives as a result. When you learn to think and act like other people who are successful, happy, wealthy, and prosperous, you will soon love the kind of life they are doing. You change your life because you change your own mindset.

CHAPTER 1

WHAT'S HEALTHY THINKING, AND WHY DOES IT MATTER?

It's possible you've thought at many times in your life that you might have a different, more optimistic outlook on things. This is a great example of wishful thinking, scolding yourself emotionally but not doing anything to consciously alter or remove those patterns that you so detest— that's a thought pit, a classic one that we'll explore later. At any point, before we get into the principles of thought loops and how good thinking impacts different types of people, we first have to ask the question: What is healthy thinking?

Yeah, in the literal sense, we can put together what it means — healthy living is thought in a manner that is good. But what does that mean in the light of our self-doubt, our pessimism that, for some, is like a virus that they don't seem to get rid of entirely. Leeching off their energies and what their motivation would be, negative thought is the leading cause of suicidal thinking, whether this pessimism is subconscious or deliberate. Pessimism can be a difficult and complex topic to discuss in and of itself, one that we will tackle later with thought loops and where they start.

What good thinking is, to be more precise, is the act of clearing your logical mind, which is reinforced by guilt, thinking that is only irrational and not rational at all, and reflecting on the truth of a

189

situation at hand. If that fact means you have to look at something in a negative light, then so be it, as long as it's as objective as possible.

As people, we have this kind of tendency to be as truthful and as right as possible whenever we are able to be. That being said, you have to recognize that you can never be truly objective when pursuing the task of becoming a better person. While we would all love to think that we can become the supreme impartial authority, our perspectives are formed by our history and our perceptions, as well as our genetics— to some extent— as so, no matter how unbiased and rational we seek to be, there will always be a bit of our perspective that bends towards one thing or another because of our individual tastes and past experiences.

That's not to say the more rational and practical plan is of course fruitless. If only you were to live your life clouded by your thoughts, just travel through life in spur after a moment's spur, simply acting on the whim of your desires, you'd probably live an unfulfilled life. Living your life by justification alone will therefore always lead to a similar conclusion, so the best course is, like so many things, the middle way between those two extremes. It's impossible not to be subtly drawn in one direction or another, and it's likely to be on the side of sentiment or logic, but what counts is the effort to be as neutral as possible considering the position. Note, however, that the object of trying to remain impartial is not so that you can be objective and apathetic to things— the point of not wanting to be influenced by intense emotion or logic is keeping you satisfied and happy as an individual.

How good thinking always means is to identify the shortcomings in your thought, and to fix those flaws while maintaining modesty and trust. It can sometimes be disheartening to have flaws in your thought pointed out to you vigorously, but it is the development that follows after that feedback that matters more than the criticism itself. It's the desire to change and become a better person that far outweighs whatever guilt you may feel when you're attacked. It's rough, sure, but it does help a lot more than it hurts.

Now, another question arises from the first — sure, positive thought seeks to become a more neutral person for the sake of inner peace, but why does that matter to any person? If I am as good as it is, then why should I worry about safe thinking?

As one thing, if you assume that your attitude is as safe and optimistic as it is, you certainly wouldn't be reading this book at all. There's also a question that comes with positivity though. As I said, the best road with many issues is the one put in the midst of two extremes. On the one hand, we sometimes think about how damaging pessimism can be for the ego and for the self as a whole, but the risks of being too positive are a matter not nearly as debated. This is also a problem that we will discuss in later chapters, but for now bear in mind that any drastic in this sense is definitely one that will emotionally hurt you in the long run.

Anyway— why does logical reasoning matter? This is a question raised by those who are either happy with themselves or those who know their way of thought is deeply faulty, but who are either too prideful or too apathetic to take that first step forward and really be involved in your own improvement.

The fact is, positive thought isn't just intended for those who thinks their behavior is too dangerous, or whose thinking has the potential to ruin them from within. Yes, positive thinking is something that can help everyone and anyone at all, irrespective of how much you believe your mind is already in "good" form, or at least not so bad that you need to read a book on how to develop it.

The brain is probably the most laborious organ in your body. It not only succeeds in making us into living, alien creatures that can communicate and breathe and eat and create communities, but it also helps us to think. Our minds not only allow us to be conscious of our own thinking processes. To some level, anyway, we grasp our own thinking processes — and are able to analyze them, break them down and make them better. Our minds cause us to be so complex creatures that we are not at Mother Nature's whim or fate to make us better, or to teach us lessons about life. We have our own ability to tell ourselves knowledge, absorb the wisdom and apply it to every aspect of our lives. This is an insane thing to think of; our brain's power, but in the first place it is that same power that helps us to think about it.

Therefore, the strength of positive thought is really the same power our brain provides us— the ability to be aware and edit ourselves anytime you really want. The strength is something that we still take for granted, assuring ourselves that our religion, or destiny, will bring us on through life and that we don't really have to rely on our own thoughts to do much. We believe that we focus much, much less, on our feelings than we really do. The emotions are not only an integral part of us as humans, but that is what makes up the meaning, our constant stream of knowledge. The only moment in our minds when we feel "silence" is when we're so focused on something that all of our emotions go on the back burner for a while. We have an almost constant stream of internal expression running into our minds for the rest of our human experience, feeding us information that perhaps we didn't even know we had access to in the first place. Some of the emotions that we hear, some of them are not yet ours. Whether those are mischievous intrusive thoughts, or just thoughts we don't really agree with, spontaneous strings of knowledge that were more impulsive and intentional, those thoughts can sometimes trigger confusion in ourselves and in our own feelings. This discord between us and our emotions that causes a divide between our physical selves and our emotional selves can be extremely problematic when it comes to communicating more closely with ourselves, our beliefs or even sharing heart-to-heart relationships with other people. When we have a poor connection with ourselves, such relations can be weakened or strained. Healthy thought can both help to make a bond better and avoid the issues that can in the first place trigger the destructive fracture.

As you can see, positive thinking is something which in many ways affects us all. It's something that can have a tremendous effect on how we perceive the world around us, how we communicate with other individuals, and it's something that has the incredible power to turn our view of the world crazy.

Getting able to think well is, so to speak, getting able to take a step back. It's the potential that we each have in all of us to take a deeper look at ourselves — a look that can simultaneously be both harshly critical and soberingly rational. Looking at things like this encourages us to act on our impulses rather than just sitting around and dwelling on them, saying to ourselves that we should act instead of waking up and taking the action. It's those same positive thoughts that not only set our plans into action but keep those plans going, keep us engaged, keep us effective, and most of all, keep us happy as well as safe.

WHAT IS ANALYTICAL THINKING?

Analytical thinking is analyzing and examining an issue or subject for the creation of more complex ideas on it. Your analytical thinking can give rise to new insights, approaches or ideas related to the issue or topic.

The process usually includes multiple steps:

- Identifying a subject, question or concern
- Collecting facts
- Developing approaches or furthering the comprehension of the situation
- Checking solutions or new ideas based on what you have heard
- Post-analysis, or evaluating what solutions succeeded, or testing your new knowledge A key element of analytical thinking is the ability to quickly find triggers This means, for example, understanding what could happen during the problem-solving process and exploring how new ideas apply to the original topic.

The bulk of analytical thinking includes both trial and error. Those with good analytical thinking skills are often able to analyze a scenario, subject or problem easily and often work well within a team setting to achieve goals.

Why are analytical skills important?

Analytical skills are important as they help you to find solutions to common issues and to determine what actions to take next. Knowing situations and evaluating the scenario for viable solutions is a crucial competency at all rates in every role. Developing this skill will improve your job, help you achieve client goals and eventually promote your personal career objectives.

If you're looking for a specific job for analytics, such as a data analyst or laboratory analyst, you should develop your industry-specific analytical thinking skills. Although analytical thinking is a soft ability, analyst positions will also allow you to have specific hard competencies relevant to the profession. This also refers to professions with the technical knowledge required such as teaching, engineering, or scientific research.

Many other professions, including computer programming, engineering, education, and customer service, include using analytical skills on a regular basis.

How to improve your analytical skills

Improving your analytical skills could help you achieve different career goals. Increasing your analytical skills on your curriculum vitae and during your interview can also help you stand out in the hiring process when applying for jobs.

Consider taking a few of the following steps to improve your analytical skills:

- Taking on leadership roles requiring the use of critical analytical skills
- Develop essential analytical skills in your current role
- Take courses emphasizing the use of analytical skills
- Participate in events involving the use of analytical skills such as team sports, gaming or reading
- Seek advice or mentoring from experts in your field or business
- Provide work on best practices for your industry
- Improve your understanding of subject matter, which is necessary for better problem-solving

Take some time to evaluate the analytical skills that you possess and those where you can develop. Write down specific times when you used analytical skills to improve something or solve a problem, whether at work, in a volunteer position or at school.

WHAT IS EGO?

The ego is our own creation identity of the soul, an identification which is false. We're more than just attitude. If we take all of the assumptions about what we are— beliefs about our personalities, strengths, and abilities— we have our ego structure. Such skills, strengths and facets of our personalities will be characteristics of our skill, but our "self" intellectual model is false. And while this definition may seem like a stagnant thing to the ego, it is not. Actually, it is an integral and complex aspect of our personality, playing an important role in our lives to generate emotional drama.

The Ego Unmasked

Why is that ego too difficult to explain or describe? The ego is hard to define, because the ego is not one particular thing. In reality, it's made up of many different values a person acquires over their lifetime. Such beliefs may be complex and even conflicting. To confuse that further, the ego of each person is special. If someone defines and explains specifically all the aspects of their ego and what it pushes them to do, you may not get a good description of what it looks like. The challenge of becoming conscious of what your personal ego feels like is getting harder because our society does not praise us for turning our focus inward and realizing these issues.

How to Spot the Ego

The ego is hard to see, because it lies behind real-life perceptions—our adherence to representations of our personality—and because we haven't practiced searching. You can glimpse other feelings, similar to those mentioned above, by observing them. The easiest way to spot the ego is through the trail of emotional reactions that it leaves behind: frustration at a loved one, a need to be perfect, a sense of vulnerability in some cases, irrational feelings of envy, the need to please someone, and so on. The false beliefs that form the ego will relate these feelings to. In the beginning the signs of subsequent feelings and stress are harder to see, rather than the personality that triggered it.

One of the ego's most troubling characteristics is that it produces powerful emotional emotions, then excuses us for how it made us feel. The indignation with which we respond stems from ego-based assumptions that we are right and' know better' than someone else. There may also be an understanding of the survivor of deception or inequality below. When we overreact with frustration we can feel bad about what we've been saying. The ego is moving to a "righteous self" that "knows better" and is advising us to overreact with frustration. Simultaneously, it assumes the reputation of being the "stupid idiot" who knows no better and takes the blame for overreacting. All of these actions, emotions, and opinions take place in the subconscious, and although they are entirely different, we believe they many come from us. If they were words that really come from our own selves they wouldn't dispute and we could save them.

To the unconscious person, the distinction between what is ego and what it really is hard to discern. They're left to wonder, "What happened to me that I had behaved like this?" And their post-emotional examination lacks the understanding of treating the various parts of their system of beliefs at work as distinct from themselves. As a result, one of the accusing voices in their head blames everything that they say on "they themselves." The ego then hijacks the study and turns it into a process of self-criticism / blame. You have no chance to see the root cause of your interpersonal tragedies when the ego dominates the self-reflection process, as the ego reaffirms itself and hides in self-criticism.

Is the ego arrogant or insecure?

"Having an ego" is usually associated with pride, and is a term used to describe someone who feels that they are stronger than others. And that's just a function of the ego. It is actually possible to have some positive self-esteem and some negative self-esteem-at different times we are mindful of these different beliefs. The pessimistic views about our self-making make up our negative self-esteem, while our positive thoughts reflect our positive self-esteem. Together, our ego shapes the negative and the positive value.

Quite often, these two facets of our personalities are almost equal in size, and morally balance each other. A person with their inner critic who is very harsh on him or herself may have feelings of worthlessness. This is a difficult emotion to deal with, and they may cover it up with bravado to disguise the pain, projecting an image of stability and loyalty, all the while coping with feelings of insecurity, worthlessness and inadequacy.

Arrogance differs markedly from the belief that doesn't come from vanity. A person can have total confidence in his ability, ability, or self-acceptance, without making him "go to his head" and having an impact on his relationships with others. And while modesty can often be mistaken for shyness and vulnerability, a person of true humility is fully present and at peace with himself and his world. Confidence without pride, modesty without fear, these are personality habits which are without the ego's self-image dynamics.

Letting Go of the Ego

Since the ego has multiple aspects, dissolving all of it at once is not realistic or successful, nor is it possible you will. Just like a tree or big bush overgrown in the yard, you're not just taking it out and throwing it away–you're carving out useful bits instead. The same method is successful in letting go of the false convictions which make up the ego. You start by detaching yourself from individual thoughts which reinforce the ego, then letting go of beliefs, removing yourself from your ego's false identity.

We have spent years creating and strengthening our self-images of personality, working behind them. It will take more than a few days to remove our true selves from that web of false beliefs. Yeah, it'll take some time...... so what. Learning to read, do math, walk and develop skills at any useful activity always took a while. It takes time and practice to get things worth doing. What better thing to do than let go of what makes you unhappiness?

CHAPTER 2

THE SUMS OF OUR THOUGHTS

Our thoughts and feelings play a massive role in the everyday way in which we live our lives as individuals more than we so often know and document. After all, the very reason we wake up in the morning is determined by our first alert, conscious thoughts. Why we do the things we do, the path in life we take on the basis of those choices, and the places we end up in, are largely decided by our constant stream of thoughts that we have to choose through every day to figure out which thoughts we hope will enable us to excel that day and on. Each idea we have, although it may seem dismissible, is something that could have produced an infinite number of past decisions and emotions. Also impulsive feelings, and the ideas that we most hate— those that we hide deep within us and try to push away in the expectation that they will never emerge and lift their ugly heads — are thoughts and expressions of our personalities that we cannot disregard. Therefore, in the long run, we cannot neglect them and still be healthy people working. Most people have all sorts of ways of dealing with their feelings, many of which they may not like. Many people choose to record their thoughts in some manner, whether through a kind of video diary or written entries — this approach allows you to express your thoughts more concretely, which in effect will allow you to address these issues more effectively and with a better objective in mind. For fact, video diary entries, or any other kind of verbalization of concerns or intrusive feelings, help clear the mind of tension or other troubles. For example, there are so many ways people go about dealing with their feelings and their problems and some try to deal with those same thoughts by avoiding them and almost slipping into a denial state.

While for some people this state of denial can succeed, most of it for at least a short while, there are very few people who can really drive a string of thoughts away forever. There are not many people in the world who can block any kind of idea for a very long time— this may be why many people say a thought that is "true" or "fated" to see the light of day will still find its way out. Despite the fact that this statement is old and fairly ambiguous, experience has seen reality. Also, when we have something we talk about it upsets us, it's generally something disturbing because either it's true or it's connected to the truth. The fact with which we have not yet come to terms is that the truth which makes us the most uncomfortable — take, for example,

Harper Lee's To Kill a Mockingbird. In early 20th century America, Lee's seminal novella of corruption, punishment, and racism is one that is heavily discussed, even today. It often tops the charts of literary works most commonly banned or written about in classrooms, most of those protests citing sexism, vocabulary of use or derogation or connection to violence as a purpose. Of course, many would say that the true reason Lee's masterpiece makes so many people so profoundly sad is because they all know, in a small part of themselves, that the book's preachings are still true for today. We have far from removing the problems so strongly touched on in the novel, and yet we now have something of a growing social problem in which one side disputes that we have eradicated the hate speech and the ignorance of people so antagonistically depicted, and the other side insists that we have not only removed the contentious and insulting subjects of the book more or less, but that the book's. The argument goes on and on as it has been for many years now, and will continue for many years, but the point that To Kill a Mockingbird and many other classic and divisive works of literature make is that the facts will always make people uncomfortable as long as that fact is one that embarrasses other people. Actually, humans are a fundamentally selfish race, doing virtually anything to satisfy their vanity, recover a weakened ego, and convince themselves and others that they are correct in any debate, regardless of the cost. Of course we want to be right by nature for happiness, pleasure, and often for recognition, from our colleagues and/or our subordinates. We both know how good it feels to be right and prove wrong if we can, to an annoying colleague. We also assume responsibility for those selfish things we do, and yet we love them. We understand what they mean about us but we should look at ourselves and judge our actions honestly and without delusion — at any rate, most of us.

Yet, what does all of this mean in the sense of balanced thinking? What that says, actually, is much easier than you might imagine. In a way, not only do our minds identify us as people but in exchange we also have the power to define our thoughts. While our emotions do have the ability to dominate our lives and our environment, we also have the same power to take hold of our own thoughts and manage them, rather than allowing them to rule us entirely. Taking control of your thoughts is quite straightforward, really— all you need to do is become self-aware to the extent where you keep up with your thoughts and feedback about those same thoughts in near real time.

The harsh truth is, we often either give ourselves too much, or too little, of the harsh truth. Actively mediating, and somehow trying to find the middle ground between the two nations, is very complicated. Each situation in which we take part, whether we are participating or simply watching on the sidelines, has a rather pronounced effect on what we do, what we say, how we behave and how we respond afterwards. Even if that occurrence is not actually extremely good or catastrophic, even the most ordinary incidents will, if only small, change the trajectory of the rest of our days. Even in the literal sense, we are affected by everything we do: spending a few extra minutes in the bathroom to contemplate the day ahead and the days ahead of you will then mean that you have less time to finish getting ready for your day, and those extra few minutes may actually end up making you late to whatever duty you may have had for that day. Even the little things that happen to us every day, you know, change the way we respond.

Of course, this also extends to more introspective situations, to more painful and gloomy situations that may involve more positive thought, emotion and healing. Imagine, you were in a car accident, for example — the collision was relatively low-speed, and no one was badly injured by the impact. Nonetheless, before starting your normal routine, you have had to take time to fully heal from the said incident. While you have, of course, had to take the time to heal emotionally from that accident, the lasting effects go far beyond the immediate. Regardless matter how long you take to heal your body, regardless matter how long it takes you to resolve the anxiety or discomfort that you may have formed of cars as a result of the incident, you probably won't always have a lasting impression, and you will change the way you react and behave when you drive, no matter how minute the shift may become over time. Also years and years later, when the accident is nothing but a remarkable recollection, it will have been an event that has forever changed the way you responded to danger on the road, how carefully you behaved while behind the wheel, and many other things in a vehicle, walking or whatever. Any kind of trauma such as this that you undergo, be it solely physical or psychological, will have a lasting impact on how you respond in the future in cases where the events are associated with your past experiences. It may become a blessing or a curse, but it is what happens, even in those with an exceptionally good memory. After all, the more you remember the incident, the more often you can remember the emotions during it. Of all those emotions that change the course of your life forever.

That does not have to be this way forever, of course. You don't just have to struggle passively while you let everything that happens around you slip you by and leave a scar you're not in charge of, but you don't have to take a back seat to your own feelings. In your thinking, you play a much more active role than you might actually think, or that it might seem. Not only are you able to control your emotions in a certain way, but you can also influence and control how you are influenced by those feelings. Of course, you'll certainly always have some idiosyncrasies that remain with you due to your past experiences, but how you view your stream of consciousness is up to you, more or less. Whether you let the perception of your emotions affect your decision forwards is up to you, based on how aware you really are of your feelings.

Self-awareness is something that most people find very difficult to do, mostly because you have to be relatively self-aware, to begin with, to establish a sense of self-awareness. In your day-to-day activities, being able to identify the wrong things in your life to seeking change and purpose can be the difference between living a fulfilling life and simply growing through the motions and wondering what you ever wanted to accomplish in your life. It's very hard to get the confidence to initiate the transition on its own, but I can honestly guarantee you that any risk you take will grow to be embraced not only by you, but by the people around you who matter for you and want good things for you. Such followers, whether they're your friends, relatives, and partner, or just a group of people online with whom you believe you're related, are likely to grow to be one of the, if not the, main driving forces behind the drive to be successful and to change your way of life and your mindset.

And yeah, it's hard to put better thinking into your everyday life. It is not only hard to get started, but it is also very difficult to keep going. You may get draining the inspiration and the energy you need to keep up, to keep pushing forward to improve the way you think, and the way you live. Only keep pushing, as it is with all things, while feeling the pressure to succeed. But — not as stressful as a life in which you exist only in the extremes, where you are always either positive and in denial or so gloomy that your perspective influences all aspects of your life. Yeah, learning how to hold your drive up for long periods of time is unbelievably difficult, but note, so to speak, that you'll have support in every corner of your ring. We'll explore the idea of "thought traps" in the next chapter —how they play in your everyday life, how you can repair them, and what they can do to you as a person on your way to changing your life and being happier and healthier.

HOW TO CHANGE YOUR THINKING

1. Change your thoughts by creating positive affirmations

Assurances aren't always optimistic. We too can be pessimistic. The hexes the witches make are pessimistic affirmations.

The reality is that most people are given pessimistic statements to make. If you constantly believe you won't be successful in a particular project, it's a pessimistic reinforcement. Affirmations, both negative and positive effects on brain neurological function.

Positive statements mimic mantras. We have a divine and holy energy about them. Let us be sure that constructive affirmations are made. We should not be low or prescriptive.

Thoughts like' shall," sought to' or' abstain from' are prescriptive.

Types of negative statements include:' I can't' do this. It's' pretty hard.' On the other, affirmations such as' I will," I should' or' I'm going to' should be strong and committed. As described above, your brain often adapts to your habits of thought, and commands your organs to act accordingly.

2. Learn to apply full stop

We keep mulling about our misfortunes, the supposed wrongs done to us by those we so deeply cherished and stood by. They never stop to blame ourselves for the errors they think we have made. And if I had done this or that, would have happened? What would happen in future if I were to do this or that?

This is not to say that we should not learn from past mistakes, or intelligently plan our future. The only thing we can stop thinking about once we've learned about our mistakes and settled on our future.

3. Let go of the need to be masochistic

We love to wallow in our suffering quite often. They enjoy creating self-punishing emotions or being gloomy and somber. Here's an example: "When I start selling candles, the sun will stop setting, people will stop dying when I start selling shrouds." I was born unfortunate. Something good happens to me ever.

Not only do these emotions have a negative effect on the psyche, but they also have an adverse effect on your physical health.

4. Change your thoughts by counting your joys and blessings

Many people take for granted their joys and riches and start grumbling about what they don't have; or when they are faced with challenges and troubles. Only speak of those less lucky than yourselves. Or, think of a situation which might have been worse than it is now. You weep because an injury has injured your leg. What, had the limb broken itself? For happiness see the full half of the bottle and the vacant half with a determination to fill it.

5. Appreciate and enjoy what you already have

Always understand and accept what you already have, is a perfect way to change your feelings. This is not to say you don't aspire to an even better life. Accept the amount of success you've gained, instead of feeling sad about what you couldn't do. Sometimes setting higher targets or goals is no mistake, but failure to reach them should not ruin the satisfaction of what you already have.

WHAT IS CRITICAL THINKING?

The ability to think logically and rationally, to grasp the logical connection between concepts, is critical thinking. Since the time of early Greek thinkers such as Plato and Socrates, critical thinking has been the subject of much debate and analysis and has continued to be a subject of discussion into modern age, such as the ability to recognize false news.

Critical thinking could be described as being capable of engaging in analytical, independent thought.

Critical thinking essentially requires you to make use of your abilities to reason. It's about being an active learner, rather than a passive learning receiver.

Critical thinkers challenge theories and conclusions rigorously, instead of taking them at face value. We will always try to decide whether the whole picture is reflected by concepts, claims and results and are open to finding that they do not.

Critical thinkers should objectively define, evaluate, and solve problems, rather than through intuition or instinct.

Someone who has critical thinking skills may:

- Consider the links between concepts.
- Determine the validity and value of the claims and ideas.

- Recognize, create and appraise claims.
- Identify inconsistencies and logic mistakes.
- Consistently and consistently resolve challenges.
- Think on why their own opinions, convictions and ideals are valid.

In certain cases, critical thinking involves thinking about things in order to arrive at the best possible solution in the situations which the thinker is aware of. It's a way of thinking about what's currently occupying your mind in more everyday language, so that you come to the best possible conclusion.

CHAPTER 3

THINKING TRAPS, OR THINKING "SANDPITS"

There are many situations in which all sorts of people can slip through conceptual traps, many of which are extremely difficult to navigate our way out of-difficult, but certainly not impossible. Nonetheless, there are a certain number of specific loopholes in which most individuals suffering persistent depression are often deeply entrenched. This article is by no means one that extends to all kinds of people, but it is a broad compilation of common "thought pits," and common ways to get out of them.

- Over generalizing a bad time — this kind of person is often a very fatalistic person, someone who has decided the worst result possible will always come to pass. When that result does not arrive, they completely ignore it, but when it does-this type of person frequently uses words like "still" and "never" to convey their belief that they are undergoing an endless cycle of horrible karma or something of that nature. This kind of person is susceptible to being influenced by the views of others about them but is also someone who is generally very direct with their own beliefs, often persuaded that opinions formed from other people's thoughts and emotions are in fact their original model. Often someone who is a pathological over generalizer often generalizes something too poorly because they want publicity or, put more simply, they want support. The theatrical style is often something like an appeal for help, an indication or desperation of a sense of helplessness they feel powerless to stop. We don't want to feel as helpless as they do sometimes, but they feel like they're always at the universe's mercy, never in control of their "fate." Like I said, they are inclined to being relatively fatalistic and are therefore never particularly inspired when it comes to shaping their fate or taking action to improve themselves — they usually feel that nothing they do is going to matter in the long run, so there is no great point in trying to do anything different when all will inevitably return to their original state. Someone who feels this kind of thought trap may feel compelled to merely lazily let themselves travel through life without any concern or connection in the universe, but they must wake up and realize that living that way would lead them to the road of unfulfillment and hollow existence. They have to be the first to get up and actually do something about it if they want to change their "life," their "destiny," their "fate" Those who constantly generalize over also consider themselves the persistent beneficiary of terrible luck. I say such things like, "this always happens to me!" In the heart, some of these people know it's not logically true, so they tell it anyway because it gives them a form of cathartic relief to feel as if they can't change their situation in any way. People who fall into negative thinking of this type are typically unified by a feeling of being a survivor. The respect and affection they so desperately needed as children were obviously not given to them, and their need for attention reflects in this way. This is not, of course, always the way that this need for recognition appears in adults. Unfortunately, often children who have been abused in their history, either by their mother or by someone else in their earlier lives, demonstrate their need for affection and comfort by imagining themselves to be the victim of almost any situation in which they are. Those who generalize this way sometimes have a resemblance to pathological liars, thinking themselves to be the perpetrator, where they may be the abuser. We need to understand and document the fact that the world has no more or less regard for them than any other human on Earth in any way, shape or form. The belief or hypothesis that they actually receive bad luck more often than others, no matter how it may seem to them, is little more than paranoia. The only thing that affects how many good or bad things happen to them is the decisions they do for themselves, or do not. There is no karmic power which will turn your life around someday. You have to be the person standing up and pushing yourself to confront the reality of a situation. Whether that fact leans on the good or the negative side, there is hardly any better medicine for those who believe they have any specialties in the universe's eyes than a strong dose of humility. The modesty will at least do something to convince them the not only do they have no actual karmic power in the world that punishes them for some random act, but they are the only thing in the universe that can lead the active role in making their lives fulfilled.

- People who think of the world as wrong and right, black and white, yes or no — these kinds of people are the types of characters that are often too harsh on themselves, and sometimes too hard on others too. We are people who want to do well but are opposed to the idea that there is some sort of grey area between two ends of a situation for whatever reason. They want an answer to every and every question, a straightforward and definite answer that is transparent and lined up in dark red ink before them. We want to be replied, not just as a figure of authority or someone with influence, but just as someone who is on an almost continual quest for knowledge and comprehension of everything and anything. We want to explain in the easiest and clearest possible terms, all we can. Using "I don't know" for a reaction is usually very difficult for them, even tougher than using "no" It's the complexity of a situation that upsets them and drives them crazy to no end. I can't stand the thought that they don't know and cannot understand the way the cogs churn in everything. These are also the kinds of people that give themselves too barely the leeway. This kind of thought also derives from strain in their youth, where they were probably a child who, in college or some other area, excelled, or was pressured to excel. The pressure to succeed, pressure that so often came in very toxic doses, became so normal for them, that they simply adopted the coping mechanism for themselves in their adulthood. Today, the black and white thinker doesn't let themselves rest in their maturity, doesn't let themselves have a break from their potentially busy— and definitely overwhelmed with different tasks and responsibilities— life, and almost certainly doesn't let themselves indulge and have a weekend off. We always have to be employed, we always have to be successful and in their own eyes they are meaningless. This is undoubtedly how they were taught by their parents or guardians— so that they become valuable when they do excel and when they do become the strongest. Yet when they are no longer the best, or when they rest or unwind, they are worthless. This kind of intense thinking comes from an incomprehension that relaxing is a very important part of efficiency. They don't know how to relax because they grew up with the idea that it was infinitely more important to be successful than being healthy, confident or satisfied. They just take the "A+" as a grade when starting a program. If they are not immediately up to their own expectations, then the whole idea is a total disaster, they are a loser, and now the thinking is worth nothing for them. This is a very dangerous way of thinking as it often drives them to cancel plans as soon as they hit the first obstacle, no matter how long or complicated it may be. As long as there is any sign of potential danger, or the slightest hint of what may grow to be that they find a mistake, they are much more likely to abandon their scheme completely than others who do not share their mentality. This is an intense, often dysfunctional habit for many people, as you can see, and it often makes people seem less attractive as mates and as partners as well. Someone who views the world solely through a strictly black and white filter will be draining to the stomach for most people, and will therefore be less enjoyable to be around than others. Treating the universe as a science project not only pressures and dehumanizes the people around the individual, it also stresses them out and can lead to the loss of their sense of identity in many instances. A diminished identity may seem like the last expected result of viewing the world too negatively, but to put it this way may be more eloquent, more simply— we, as people, have an identity more or less determined by our emotions and experiences. If you do all you can to remove the "gray area" that feelings generate in contexts, and therefore restrict the cognitive capacity of your interactions to just the actual, realistic, surface-level interpretation, you will lack the credibility that your emotions once so carefully cultivated over time. Such types of people are best suited to conditions in which they are required to adapt, in terms of improvement. Someone who's generally too hard on themselves and others need to know how to find a balance and realize that they don't have to give into their intense compulsions. When they understand the dangers and long-term disadvantages that life can have in this manner, people who look at stuff like this are more likely to loosen up and take advice from others, as well as consider a touch of grey for every black and white human.

- The cynical fortuneteller— this is someone who's recognized for someone who's constantly forecasting the future, and who's always likely to blow in their face for that prediction. The fortune teller may take as many positive steps towards their target as they like, but they still find themselves falling prey to the voice in their head that warns them that no matter what, in all their efforts they are doomed to suffer a loss of a disappointment. Such kinds of forecasts frequently lack overwhelming facts, and yet they somehow find a way to twist virtually every story against them, even when they don't actually want to. This kind of person comes under the umbrella more or less that the over-generalizer is also frequently found under, as the two are very close in their defeatist attitude. The main difference between the two styles lies in the fact that while most people who over-generalize were once adolescents starved of love so that by victimizing themselves they are now finding some satisfaction, the fortuneteller doesn't necessarily seek that affirmation from others as much. Alternatively, fortunetellers respond as a child to a lack of attention and love by internalizing the disrespect. The over-generalizer thinks they have been mistaken by not being given the respect they feel they deserve, while the fortuneteller believes it is much more likely that they deserve the lack of recognition. By not being granted consideration they don't necessarily feel guilty, since they believe the injustice was warranted more than not. While the over-generalizer thinks terrible things are going to happen to them because they sound like the world is out to get them, the never-upbeat fortuneteller has a bad habit of always convincing himself they are always being set up for failure. The difference lies in where these two forms assume that the antagonism stems from. While the former kind firmly believes that there is some supernatural force that relentlessly sabotaging them and their dreams, the latter kind of individual is far more likely to believe that they are the ones who destroy themselves. This fortuneteller considers themselves to be someone who deserves their own misfortune, and they expect it to continue far into the future. Any bad thing that happens to them now only leads to their firm conviction that they are the perpetual victim of their own negative qualities. Not only that, but the cynical fortuneteller thinks they are disproportionately inferior to those around them, sometimes assuring themselves and sometimes even others that they really don't have what it takes to succeed in whatever they seek. We firmly believe we are destined to fail not because of the flaws in the cosmos or some divine fate, but because of their own shortcomings. Instead of generalizing the way things only "seem" to happen to them, they generalize their way of acting and behaving in order to paint themselves as useless. Like most styles on these lists, the fortuneteller almost always has a damagingly low self-esteem, and so seeking the emotional comfort they are hoping for extremely difficult. Occasionally, these people's best escape is just going to therapy and sorting out their problems with the help of a therapist who knows how to treat them. For example, if professional help is out of the picture— whether that is because the condition is not serious enough, or the person in question simply refuses to see a psychiatrist or some other form of approved aid— any strategies that often benefit people with a similar problematic problem include replacing the bad behavior with another. Occasionally, those who want to get rid of unwanted or uncomfortable mental tics or repetitive feelings, snap themselves with a rubber band or have some other kind of mind but not torturous physical punishment imposed on them, either by themselves or by another human, if they slip up and fall back into the habit. To many, this is an unorthodox approach but it certainly works well for most people. Alternatively, for those with the willpower, they can find positive affirmations that take the place of time that otherwise would be spent putting themselves down. For example, if you hear something like "I know I've done well, but I'll actually either mess up or lose somehow," contradict yourself— either out loud or to yourself— and say something positive to overcome the negative feeling. Even if it sounds slight or excessively stupid, and the positive feeling conveyed to you on a regular basis over a period of time will show results in your life and mind. Doing such things over and over again will increase your self-esteem and motivation over time. Of course, like all recovery, it's a slow process, but when you start experiencing life outside of your thought pit, whatever effort you have to do to live in that position becomes more than worth the trouble.

- Emotional reasoning — a completely different type of mental sandpit, and one that is just as unhealthy and dangerous, but for a whole different set of reasons. Simply put, emotional reasoners find a way to let their emotions— that is, their fears— take over their thinking, keeping them away from what could be a peaceful, safe environment. Most men, for starters, are afraid of heights, aircraft or the ocean. Persons who have this anxiety and an emotional thinking pattern may conclude that those areas are logically dangerous if they feel anxious when they are out on the beach, in an airport, or at a high place. This kind of thought can really hinder what a person can do, whether it means that they can make their travel plans unnecessarily long and boring, or never get a decent chance to enjoy the beach at all. People who think like this may also have a propensity to victimize themselves and thus often ruin other people's fun of things. It does not come from a very malevolent place, like all the other forms on those lists, but it comes from a buried desire place. Of course the need is for attention and care. Those who victimize themselves like that were always once young living in a household that had some sort of unspoken social code. We often have no way to vent their feelings, and fear adequately because they have never before been able to share them. So now that maturity encourages them to express their feelings, they have no idea how to reconcile their reasoning and their emotions. But, since they have such a negative connotation with using their logic and reasoning, it is often difficult to find a balance because people like this sometimes face difficulty in using their regular reasoning. That can make them feel like they have to use their emotions to make up for "lost time" at almost all times today. This habit may or may not be involuntary but it is a habit that affects many people in various ways. For simplicity's sake, I'm explaining all the different types of traps of thought and people who suffer from them in very drastic terms. Many people don't really feel this way about their feelings or their fears, but for a fairly long time this is something that lingers inside them. The way to get rid of this habitual emotional-logical paradox? Exposure therapy. Like many of the people who suffer from these loops of thought, emotional reasoners believe that there is some sort of bad spiral that is either triggered by or associated with those events that give them distress. Ideally, they need to be shown that these things aren't dangerous at all, and are just really fun when you can calm down and let yourself think your way out of the anxiety spiral. If they can finally feel comfortable in an environment where they would normally feel lots of stress and anxiety, the possibility of having to endure such problems will be more accessible to emotional reasoners. This also helps them to use their logic and reasoning, rather than just using their emotional response— their knee-jerk response— to anything that causes them discomfort or makes them uncomfortable. It will support an emotional reasoner, of course, to have a partner with them when they go through one of those stressful moments. Getting a close "voice of reason" will help them feel at home and practice their reasoning skills to get them out of their own heads.

- Negative labeling— these kinds of people are most commonly found in an office or high school today. Some kinds of people don't know how to get positive attention from others correctly, so they mark themselves outwardly as derogatory. Negative labelers, however, often have difficulty labeling those around them as simply their negative qualities. Simply put, the negative labeler is typically a person who has been unfairly branded throughout much of their life. Often we see that when used to them, people who view us unfairly and see the world in his kind of cut and paste, black and white lens were first introduced to that spectrum. Throughout their youth they were undoubtedly surrounded by people who looked at life in a similar manner, blaming others and themselves for their suffering, but doing nothing to personally try and stop it. That sort of laziness is also often only attributed to whoever they claim that way in their past actions. The aggressive labeler, as children so often do, just picks up where that person left off in their youth, acting the way they do because it's the only way they know how to handle these kinds of issues. Compared to the "black and white" form in section one, pessimistic labelers also have a tendency to see things in a very cut and dry way. Some people want things to go their way, or else the fault lies with little to no guilt either in the other side or themselves. We learn how to criticize themselves but not how to solve the problem by doing anything constructive about it. This happens in a lot of people— they have a kind of defeatist mentality, yet they do nothing to stand up and get actively involved in changing anything or making a better decision. We let it go until it comes back and hits them hard enough to drive them out of their chair because we believe they have done something wrong. To negative labelers a simple solution is to force them into being more positive about their lives. Since they take their own decisions so often with a back seat, they may not realize what it is like to take responsibility and repair it. The question also arises when people let their failures go after they let threats fly— when they do nothing to solve the problem, they not only let the problem go free, but they also let their relationships with others deteriorate when they do nothing to restore them. Such people need a tough wake-up call, something bad to happen to them and someone to be up front with them, remind them that if they just corrected their initial mistake, such bad things wouldn't happen to them! What pessimistic labelers might assume is a relentless loop of negative events is really a cycle of events that sprang from their original fault, which will now come back and bite them over and over again. Negative labelers are individuals who, until something serious happens, are unable to do anything about their condition and what constitutes "bad" for them will vary from person to person.

- "Should have, could have, would have" statements— this kind of pit of thought happens mostly in individuals who are not opportunistic, but may wish they could be more like that. Those who often fall into this pit believe that they are inferior or that they do not reach their full potential because they do not deliver on their desires, yet they do not act on them. This sort of thought pit, somewhat similar to the derogatory labeling method, often does not necessarily inspire the person in question— it only drives them deeper and deeper into their hole of self-doubt, without motivating them to do anything about it. This is because not only does this kind of thought lock the individual into the illusion of what might have been and set them up for disappointment by setting their expectations far too high for themselves, but it also puts them in the frame of mind that they are helpless or too fragile to do the acts they desire, or say the things that are most on their minds. We believe we have to act in a certain way, that this is the only way to accomplish their goal, and they don't open their eyes to the rewards of what they did. People who fall into this trap of thinking usually have a lot of trouble letting go of the past and making peace with their choices, sometimes suffering from the sense that "grass is always greener," assuming their life would be different, and stronger if they had taken completely different decisions. Occasionally, they may or may not realize instinctively that this is simply not true, that it wouldn't change their present state at all, no matter what they had done in the past. Nonetheless, people who fall into this kind of trap of thinking, or pessimistic spiral of emotion, generally always feel anxious and discouraged about their own past choices. The best way to defeat this kind of reasoning is to push them to avoid thinking about the past, and their actions. Therefore, reflecting instead on the moment is the best way to counteracting the feelings of regret. Instead of worrying only about the previous decisions they have made and the impact they have on them, they should focus their attention on the decisions they have immediately in front of them or near ahead. We also hyper-focus on the regrets of their life we have about past decisions, when instead they could focus on bringing more consideration and careful deliberation into their management decisions. If you concentrate on the things that you can influence, you will end up with significantly fewer regrets in the future. Positive affirmations often support when faced with regret and sadness about a choice that you may have felt was taken in poor taste. Even though you can't change the decision you've made in the past, there are always ways you can overcome the change you've made in your and other lifetimes. Not only can you focus on making better choices from now on, but you can also try to correct the effects that your bad choices have made on your life and on others' lives. Showing you want to improve will not only allow others to forgive you, but will also support you to form relationships that you may have missed from those bad choices. In fact, for those who struggle from this sort of remorse, keep in mind that although your choices are irreversible and cannot be reversed in and of themselves, you have the power to control where you ultimately take those decisions. You can monitor how you respond to circumstances that throw your way, and you have the power to change your life course even more than you might expect.

- Mind reader— this type of person is often, somehow, incredibly confident and nervous at the same time. People seem to have such incredible faith in their perceptions of the world around them and the people with whom people communicate, yet all these predictions rely on them. It's normal for you to find people who act in this way, somehow too confident in their abilities at the same time, but only in their abilities that promote negative self-consciousness. Like many of the styles on this list, the mind reader has an incredibly low amount of self-esteem, and so seeks other people's approval and encouragement by stating their negative views of themselves as a fact, or at least as contrary to be. Unlike some of the more hyperbolic forms, like the labeler, their cynical view of the world is not imposed on others by the mind reader. The cynical labeler will return to offending others to justify their own failures or mistakes; the reader in mind simply assumes that people speak about them poorly. Often this "mind-reading" has very little to do with their assessment of the people there. In reality, they frequently find themselves celebrating individuals that they expect think poorly about. We consider all other negative treatment as benefits, as if they are serving an eternal criminal sentence in a past life for their actions. This kind of low self-esteem most often stems from a home life of neglect, or even violence, often mental and emotional— although in most abusive homes, physical and verbal abuse is not often found without one another. Therefore, those who suffer from this kind of thought pit may potentially be best suited for professional help, like counseling, in most serious cases at least. Finding someone licensed to help them get through whatever depression they might have can sometimes be the strongest, or only, the person's road to breaking free from that self-loathing filled loop. We still find it difficult to see the bright side of life, at least for themselves, and really struggle to think of themselves as the norm in the sense that they are "good enough." Whether that means pretty enough, clever enough or tough enough, the mind reader frequently views themselves as exceedingly inferior to their friends and even strangers, about whom they often don't know. We presume the worst of themselves and often take on the best of others. We usually know this way of thinking is wrong, not to mention dangerous, but we lack the confidence and courage to believe enough in themselves to do anything about it. Some of them believe they are always going to be compared to their superiors, and to everyone around them. Whatever influenced them earlier in their lives to make them believe they are terrible people, or just people who will never be deserving of their achievements, accomplishments, or whatever they do some people may find important, or worthy of praise, they believe the influence from others will always be with them, now a part of them resolved never to leave. For some people, it really never does — they turn their trauma as part of their coping mechanism, and drown in cynical pessimism their frustration and worries, thinking they will never improve and life will never get better to them. The best medicine for people who, as I said, are suffering from this kind of thought pit is counseling, which is preferably done beforehand with a support system. Sometimes people who feel that way, who believe they're being manipulated and disliked by everyone around them, need to learn to trust people again before they can erase their critical thinking process. Treatment is typically an excellent way to build up the ability to forgive yourself and trust people around you again. You are not despised for people who feel they may come under the "mind reader" category. You are plenty, and always will be enough.

- Mental filter— a more general description of many different types of people suffering from many different types of thought loops, those with a perceptual barrier or, more simply, a toxic filter, does not automatically perceive the world in a distorted or deluded way. Unlike the mind reader kind, people don't think wrong things about the negative filter. Despite knowing the facts of their situation they don't believe the worst of things and people. Rather, those with a pessimistic filter almost entirely ignore positive aspects of things, or their condition, depending on the severity of their question. People also focus solely on the negative sides of an issue, concentrating on what makes them feel depressed, irritated, alone, frustrated or otherwise placing them in a

poor mind frame. This can be for any reason —
sometimes, as with many of the other forms, it is a result
of negligence in the person's past. Sometimes the former
protector of the victim had that same pattern of dwelling
only on the negative, and as an infant, the person simply
followed suit, as a child does. Sometimes the habit grows
clearly on its own, sometimes when the individual has an
attitude of contrary. What I mean is that often when a
person deliberately puts on a negative attitude that was
not explicitly or at least partially caused in the past by
their surroundings, the attitude is mostly embraced in the
first place because the person in question is mostly
irritated. We are hell-bent on being isolated from the
mainstream, and thus pursue a much more cynical world
view. You might believe you're deluding yourself into
thinking the world is better than it actually is when you
reflect on the positive side of a situation. It creates almost
a kind of fallacy because, then, the person in question
turns to the opposite extreme and adopts such a
pessimistic perspective that they are themselves deluded
into thinking the universe is worse than it really is. This
edgy way of looking at the world is normal and gradually
evolves into a process of which the individual is often not
even really conscious. So, the habit of pessimism chips
away at the individual day after day as they become a

cynic, unable to form positive thoughts and eventually become a melodramatic shell of their previous self. That's not always the case, of course, for people who look at the world this way. Occasionally, it can evolve from a fear of illusion. People who develop behaviors like this often believe that they are being fooled in some way by being positive. This delusion grows until the individual becomes pathologically pessimistic to the point that, again, they actually follow the opposite side of the spectrum, being deluded into the belief that something bad will happen to optimistic people, and that this occurrence will break their hope and leave them shattered. Apparently the truth is quite the reverse. Those who are more cynical are more likely to be negatively impacted by traumatic or even traumatizing incidents over the long term. On the opposite, those with a more hopeful, confident outlook on life are more likely to be affected in the short term, but because of their positive attitude — ensuring, of course, that this positive attitude remains intact and relatively unchanged after that incident— they will recover quickly and recover further, whilst their negative equivalents seem more to keep on to stuff for an event For example, this can cause a lot of trouble for pessimists, because they are often disillusioned to think they have the upper hand. It comes from the misunderstanding between pessimism and rationality, which later chapters will go into more detail. Pessimism derives from the anticipation of the worse, while optimism has no hope. That disparity plays a central role in how pessimists respond to issues. The best way to "treat" this kind of mind loop is to make sure they stay on the positive side of things as much as possible. Those with a pessimistic outlook on their life often don't understand that things aren't always bad and that being positive doesn't matter. Furthermore, because people with this kind of buffer realize that their condition does not improve if they become more constructive — even if their situation gets improved with this adjustment in perception — they are often far more likely to continue to be more optimistic in the long run.

CHAPTER 4

ESCAPING THE THINKING SINKHOLE, SANDPIT, AND COMMON TRAP

The number of ways in which you believe you can 'go wrong' is enormous and multiple. Perhaps there are too many ways you can go wrong with your thinking, it's about time we discuss the many directions you can change your steps, and go right with your thought instead. So don't worry, it's easy as long as you're reliable.

If working with something of your own making, consistency is the key. If you aren't pushed into something, you need to develop your own power. Unfortunately, the momentary burst of passion and excitement doesn't last forever, especially for someone who doesn't consider themselves to be very exciting people. Nonetheless, you have to replace slow and steady determination with that excitable action and passion. Being diligent in your actions in life also contributes to the satisfaction of the tests. As a wise man once said: "Ambition is the path to greatness. Persistence is the vehicle which you arrive there in." Now that we've been over the different kinds of thought traps that are most common in today's world in more depth, it's important to understand how best to get out of those traps. Although yes, I've explained some of the more specific things about some of the various pitfalls, as you come to terms with your thought loop, here are some of the more common choices for you.

- Separating your thoughts from reality— as I briefly mentioned in the previous chapter, there really is a huge difference between pessimism and optimism. While yeah, clearly pessimism is to look at things in a negative way and optimism is to look at the beginning reality with both its ups and downs, there's a bit more to it. Pessimism, for one thing, draws all its assumptions from looking at things in a negative light. This draws its conclusions from negative assumptions about the environment and the interactions within it. Meanwhile, there is really nothing reality has to draw conclusions from on its own. Ideally, a realist makes no assumptions other than observations and conclusions that could have been drawn without using human error or partiality. Realism, in a perfect example, uses only factual information and the objective evidence truth to answer questions on that reality. Of reality it is impossible to completely eradicate any human error or prejudice, but preferably, when making an assessment, a realist tries their best to remove any previously existing prejudices. Many people who struggle with thought loops suffer the most because their beliefs and facts are so distant. The disconnection could have resulted from many different places, from abuse in the past to childhood deprivation to a variety of many different things that might have happened in the person's past, but if you're someone struggling to get out of a thought bind and want to attempt to reconcile the truth of your world and your experiences in it, ask yourself some of the following questions when you start" By presenting facts and information that anyone who has observed or engaged in the incident will agree unequivocally without reservation or inference," What do I think?" Analyzing the cognitive process of reasoning, what you're telling yourself, dissecting your feelings so that you can actually tell the difference between the reality of a situation and the conclusions you make based on your past experiences or prejudices that you had before you were put in the scenario," How do I feel?" Analyze your emotions and the impact your thoughts have on your emotional state, learn to distinguish your thoughts from your feelings so that you don't misinterpret them, so that you can make more rational decisions based on unreliable information that you believe is real, but don't know is true, and' How am I coping with that?" Analyze your coping mechanisms to make sure that you are as healthy as possible as you cope with it. Your coping mechanisms may include removing yourself from others so as not to misrepresent your view of the encounter or case, taking deep breaths and relaxing yourself emotionally so that your feelings become more manageable as a result, and relying on your support system to only provide you with knowledge that is impartial and trustworthy, rather than further indulging in the thought pit that induces you It's also important to examine and consider how you actually react to different circumstances as you talk about how you cope with a scenario. Before you even begin to make mistakes and collapse, knowing yourself properly and how you react to things can be a huge stepping stone for you, in terms of helping to better control your potentially dangerous urges.

- Identify your thinking trap— What could be the most important step toward managing your emotions and feeling more positively is to understand why you think the way you do negatively. In other words, one of your first and most critical moves must be to figure out which of the thought loops you associate with most. The method will take a long time before you can definitely say which of the mental loops you consider to be the one you suffer most from, but a simple way to reach the most accurate conclusion is to write down your thoughts as you have them while coping with a specific tension or emotionally strenuous circumstances. When you can better understand which of your thought processes is the most regular and pervasive to you— or, in most instances, which spiral is the most troublesome in your life— you will equate the thought process to the thinking traps mentioned in previous chapters, and see which one you most associate with. Consider where you came from, as well. If you can understand what made you feel pessimistic in the specific way you do in your past, if anything, you will better understand how those negative experiences as a youth or in your childhood would have consequences in your adulthood and correspond with your particular thought pit. Of example, someone who grew up in a particularly competitive or otherwise cutthroat household where you were forced to achieve and excel, such characteristics may come back in the form of strict pragmatism in your adult life, which could manifest negatively in the form of an attitude of "black and white thinking." Note that no two people are exactly the same, so it's highly unlikely you'll encounter a thought pit the same way other people do. A person who has a particular affinity to a negative way of thinking may not fit the typical trend for most people who share the particular trap of thought. This does not make any particular person who shares a thought trap with that thinking trap less or more true in their thinking trap or in their battle with it.

- Challenge your thinking trap— That seems a little too simple to many people, but it's incredibly important to criticize whatever thought-provoking pit you believe you fail the most or have the most trouble fighting your life. While this is somewhat simple, the most important thing about overcoming the thought patterns is remaining committed to fighting them. When asked about thought pits, something many people trip about is that perhaps the most enticing sin known to man is sloth, to be idle. Why would you make an effort to battle something when some of you are so insistent that you can never really get rid of it, no matter what? When part of you know deep down that you're never going to be left with the negative part, what's the point of even trying first? Those are exactly the kinds of ideas you need to know how to isolate yourself from reality before you can start fighting your mental pit. One of the best ways of fighting the pit of thought is simply working in the opposite direction. For starters, if you're a sort of "mind reader," someone who often believes that everybody you've met with dislikes you, in order to fuel your self-loathing, battle the pattern in your thinking by continuously casting doubt on it. Although this may sound counter-intuitive, and it is important to try to invalidate certain negative thoughts as soon as they appear in your head for many of the other forms. This way, doubting certain feelings will become second nature after long enough, just as much as the conclusions were in the first place. Once it becomes so much easier to cast doubt on those feelings because they surface in your head, the next step would be to struggle against the pessimistic perception and to argue. Sometimes, casting doubt is just not enough if the person suffers badly enough from that sort of thinking. If this is the case, and no matter the pit of thinking, battling and struggling against the negative thoughts as much as possible is crucial, moving in the opposite direction to undermine those thoughts. Here are some other things to do while battling the traps in thinking;

- Examination: Take a sharper eye to the bad things you think. The more pessimistic the thinking that emerges in your mind, the more attention that should come under it. The aim here is to make it more stressful on you mentally to have a negative thought than to have a positive one, while people who have such thoughts will just let them pass as natural quite always. The aim is to make the connection between mental analysis and getting such negative thoughts in the first place, so that having those thoughts becomes more hassle than its worth, and the thinking becomes less and less regular.

- Scrutinizing your double-standard: Tell yourself if you'd say the things you do about yourself about others who are close to you. Understand that you and your worth's negative thoughts are anomalous and damaging to yourself and your mental state. Contrast yourself to others in a way that would make you more empathic with yourself, rather than criticizing yourself aggressively out of habit. This approach is made primarily for those who struggle most from a thought pit that requires very harsh self-criticism, such as the thinker "black and white" or the sort of "mind reader" Understanding to distinguish the feelings you have about yourself from reality will allow you to be able to empathize with yourself in the future and become just a little bit more naive to yourself.

- Surveying peers and equals— this form works well particularly for the sort of thought trap "should have, could have, would have." Wherever you have an unwelcome question about whether or not your thoughts and actions are good enough for you, this method involves observing. So, after the idea has been noticed, go around to those you know don't have your issues and remind them what you're having trouble with. For example, if someone has problems with a child or a particular type of job assignment, they may say "good parents / better workers can't have that kind of problem for themselves! I'm not a good worker / parent because I have this problem. "But, it's very often the reverse is entirely true. Usually, whether you question someone who you see as the epitome of what you're trying to be, or like you're failing relative to what they actually think of your case, or how they're really stacking up next to you, you're likely to be surprised by the results— because more often than not, you're the one who's deluded into thinking you're not given a chance against others, or pale in comparison. Understand that almost everybody is going through the same very same challenges. Everyone is different but most people can interact through their experiences. Keep this in mind when you have a feeling that feels like "I'm not as nice as this person or that person," because, like you, it's highly likely that they are the ones who are struggling. You have a lot more in common with your colleagues than you actually would think.

- Conduct your own experiment— we also think of those negative thoughts as a rule of law. We don't consider the possibility that these ideas we've got are impossible. So, try it for yourself next time you're having a string of thoughts around the same subject. Of example, many people have recurring fear that their friends are only really dealing out sympathy on them, or that they feel bad of them. We don't feel like they really know about those friends. Now, they're checking those ideas and texting as many mates as they can to try and make arrangements. Since they were presumably of the opinion that most, if not all, of the friends would refuse the invitation or make an excuse not to follow up, they would definitely be pleasantly surprised when more of the friends accepted the extended invitation than they expected.

Coming out of a pit of thought is in and of itself a daunting task. It certainly isn't unlikely, however. Not for you, or anybody else. Make sure that you are really linking your problems back to you when discussing the thought traps. Sometimes when we don't seem to be able to deal with our challenges or worries of our life, we dissociate ourselves from them and relate these questions instead to a fictional "someone else." In some cases this can help a lot , particularly when you need to make sure your viewpoint is accurate or you need a second opinion. Still, however, we find this is not the case when we need to re-ground ourselves and own up to our own problems. This coping mechanism will quickly turn into a cowardly crutch that lets us comfortably withdraw from our problems. And, when you sit down and try to find a way out of your thought loops, remember that even if you're not alone, nobody can better understand the problems than you can. You must be the one who determines what you, as a human, need. The qualities you are learning by taking a closer look at yourself will most likely come into play and support you later.

CHAPTER 5

HOW THESE THOUGHTS COME TO BE

We get so caught up about what, by nature, these mental loops and unhealthy ideas are, and how to get out of them, but we hardly think deeper about them— where do these thoughts really come from, to continue with? How can such an abnormal pattern of thoughts and actions persist in a person for so long while remaining completely unchecked, even until it is on an extreme level?

In reality, that answer can lie in how we raise our babies. Let me explain a little more: while many people know that one of the many topics you just "just don't speak" to others is how to raise a child "properly." While there is certainly huge debate surrounding this topic, and while for a very good reason it is such a touchy topic, there is something to be said about, maybe, how profoundly awkward this topic makes many of us feel to be debating.

It's hard to raise a child— one of the few things that are universally agreed upon as being a mom. Not only is it complicated, but there is no real solid clear way of raising a child the right way. It is ridiculous to even argue that there is a right way at all, to many. Yet, there are many ways the majority believes that there are poor ways to raise a child. One of those is allowing a parent's bias to negatively impact the infant.

To put it more simply, my mother is working towards a condition with her children where her faults are lacking — she wanted to raise children who knew what she was doing wrong, her shortcomings and benefited from them. Most parents think this way, trying to improve the lives of their kids by somehow encouraging them to both follow in their footsteps and avoid them altogether. "Take like I mean, not like I do," to be more succinct. That is to say, where many parents "go wrong," by the expectations of many other parents, is when they encourage their own vices to take root in their children.

A lot of kids are born in a very competitive environment, for example. Not only can this be anomalous with a certain kind of discipline, it can also be disruptive and even risky to the infant. Kids sometimes fail to understand the meaning behind something forced on them by a parent— young children, often, understand only the fact and the action. Children don't really know or even understand the reason an adult views them in a certain manner, children just remember the way they've been handled and on that basis make assumptions about themselves, others and the world as a whole. As such, the decisions they make affect the way they mature and act as children, and later in their life as adults. Therefore, if they draw an inference about them that is negative depending on how they were handled at school, and how the atmosphere, the community, of their childhood, are the bad patterns that originate in that child's fault indeed entirely? If that is what happens to that boy, does even matter the reason behind that upbringing? The answer to this question, in my personal experience, is "no," but that's up for debate.

Therefore, we have to wonder now, is a dysfunctional girl unstable only because of her upbringing? Is it just and always the guardian's fault that a child is the way they are? Yet, perhaps more critically, why are children making such dangerous decisions, and why are they later creating what we now perceive as chains of thinking and toxic behavior?

To go back to that scenario, let's presume you have a friend named Isaac, who was born his entire life in a very competitive environment for example. His home life was not only competitive-it was nothing short of cutthroat. He was made to feel devalued and insignificant because he struggled to excel and adhere to his parents ' expectations. Your friend Elijah was very rarely allowed to run around and play outdoors, because of such a strong insistence on performance in all fields. We weren't allowed to hang out with their peers, play games, or have a lot of what we'd deem a normal childhood or a lot of a childhood.

So, take a step back and think for a moment about that example: how do you think this kind of atmosphere would impact your friend in the long run of their lives? How would that childhood— or lack of it — influence their adulthood, and how they functioned socially after that sort of education?

Jumping back into the fray of that case, your friend Elijah has now grown into something of an introvert, even though he tries hard to connect with his peers and make friends. It just doesn't seem to work out for him and he doesn't seem to realize why. He gets upset that he doesn't seem to be able to get in touch with people he wants to get along with and make plans with. On another note, Elijah struggled with recognition and rivalry much in his adulthood. He has a significant competitive streak, one that comes mostly from his parents and his earlier years. Furthermore, this competitive streak will gradually grow from a friendly but tough attitude to someone who really can't lose to someone else physically. If he fails everything he tries at — that is, everything— Elijah obviously gets upset and feels dejected. Even the most insignificant of defeats, he takes against him as a personal slight and because of that, he feels betrayed by the people around him. On top of that, he thrives off of support from any direction that comes to him, especially people he looks up to and loves. The undying need for that affirmation is more or less what pushes him to be productive, though he acknowledges that for him and the peers this way of thinking is incredibly unhealthy. While he needs to be stronger and have a greater self-esteem, he is bound to his success by his self-worth. He acknowledges that this isn't safe at all, but he doesn't seem to be able to find any other way to measure his personal worth. Neither does his ambitious career help — it just brings him further and further down to the belief that all he does is to appease a higher authority figure. He goes further and further down the rabbit hole every time he indulges those desires. He says that he wants to stop feeling this way, because he gets little or no pleasure from it, even if he helps someone. The surge of gratification that he gets to satisfy someone is a temporary sensation, which will quickly be replaced by the desire for more, bigger, greater. Often because of his reckless actions he drives himself far too hard and experiences physical consequences.

If any of that sounds like either you or someone you know, you or a loved one are likely to suffer from an incredibly common form of thought, one that has arisen more and more over the past decade or so. Most parents follow a sort of a hybrid between a parent of a helicopter and a parent of the Drill Sergeant Type: a kind of parent who watches over their child but only in the way a teacher supervises their pupil. This kind of parent takes the technique of erasing your child's flaws to a whole new, extreme level. In trying to teach and encourage their child to be the best and stronger versions of their parents, they have given their child a whole new set of issues and challenges which they will have to deal with later in life. When all you know about learning and graduation in your childhood and you know that achieving high grades and studying a lot makes your father or guardian happy and proud, you quickly learn how to put these two things together. If you're only used to feeling like a good child when you're academically successful, what hope do you really have of growing up into a well-rounded adult? Absolutely, none. Your chances of growing up and being able to accept your failures and your faults without getting upset with yourself and others is none the slim. Of course, the blame for that rests with the parent who — sometimes unintentionally, but nevertheless — instilled in you as a young child that it is to be successful for them to be worth someone as an individual. That kind of philosophy translates well into their schooling, as most forms of education follow a similar model of thought. The very same children who lived their lives in fear of being unproductive and thus unloved thrived in that system of education. The relationship between them and their education only further strengthened the connection between their importance and their academic achievements. In a way, we have to draw the line and ask ourselves whether or not this success is really worth it in our children, from both a realistic and a spiritual perspective.

On the one side, sometimes quickly burn out those kids who are pushed so hard all their lives. Children are often viewed as special cases, children who surpass any of their more "normal peers." Because of this special treatment, many of these kids have the idea in their heads that they are not just superior in some inherent sense than those peers, but they are also indoctrinated into believing that this distinction between them and the rest of the world is going to exist for ever. As they get older, when this theory comes crashing down around them, it can have terrible effects on their emotional health and performance as well. Coming at it even from the viewpoint of someone who wants to raise a kid who is educated and successful above all else, wouldn't it be much better— both for the parent and the child in question — to raise a child who can maintain himself and take good care of his health, both physically and emotionally? It has been proven time and time again that people who learn how to manage themselves job-wise and in all other areas of their lives are shown to be more competitive across all fields and at the same time more likely to be successful and happy, a task that becomes even harder to achieve when you are so focused on your career that you completely disregard pleasure. Therefore, also with the selfish goals of this kind of parent, it works in both their favor and the youth's favor to raise a child who is well-rounded enough to take care of himself and understand how to manage the importance of his satisfaction and how much he needs, and also to understand the importance of self-gratification rather than being out of the admiration of figures of authority,

On the other hand, we will approach parenting the child from the viewpoint of a caring and compassionate parent who knows that joy actually fulfills a child more than being successful, and that this satisfaction translates into their adult lives even better than mere success, in particular the sense of individuality that so often escapes us as we get. The reason that some kids get about the feeling is that it comes from the fact that as kids they are far above their peers. We may be in elementary school and reading at a high school level, or even reading at college level. The further you go into life, though, while embracing your talent as inevitable and doing nothing to improve it further, the more your peers — many of whom are learning and constantly improving their skills to keep up with everyone else— catch up with you. Everyone reads at high school or college level soon enough and you are now an ordinary example of a reader. You avoid being the poster child of academic success and slip off the top rank. This sense of mediocrity drives for children a curious change in self-perception: what used to be a child with a complex of dominance is now a child with a complex of rather extreme inferiority. The two contrary circumstances don't always balance out, and sometimes they just tend to coexist within this person who somehow wants to be flawless and all right away as they pick it up, and also thinks dangerously poorly of themselves. The odd dichotomy of grandeur and self-loathing also fits together to form some of the chains of thinking that we often see and explored in previous chapters.

Of course, there are other ways in which the manner a father treats his offspring will strongly influence the way children act when they grow up and become an independent adult. Sometimes you see parents who are behaving in a way that is totally contradictory to that stern and rigid parent, a parent who is not only constantly acting on their child, but is also constantly acting to protect their child from any danger that comes their way. While this protective behavior may come in handy when the child is simply just a survivor and/or in danger, if it takes the form of not only that particular kind of circumstance, but also situations where the child is the target of abuse, or otherwise to blame for the penalty that they would get without the intervention of the parents. Refusing to allow your kid to view the world in a way that is realistic enough to let them learn from their mistakes essentially opens up a world of opportunities for the kind of abuse that may eventually become their newest habit. Of example, many kids who are let off the hook of things they actually did wrong when their parents interfered, now have the idea in their minds that they can get away with much more than they had originally thought, without penalty, since their parent or guardian originally allowed them to. Of example, parental involvement can counteract that, but the more a child has that connection made and unregulated in their head, the easier the pattern is to undo. This allows the child to behave entirely as they wish with little to no consequence on their conduct. We become devious and cynical, and in some situations can even become abusive. Nonetheless, this is most certainly not the child's fault, not completely at least — no, in this situation, to blame we will look to the adult, who permitted their child to do whatever they wished with their actions without repercussions. The adult who unwittingly gives their child a complex of gods, encouraging them to wreak havoc if they so wish because they know for a fact that nothing is going to happen to them, regardless of what they do or do. This form of parenting will severely damage the child when he or she becomes an adult, both in the sense of his or her social ability and the real productivity. If you feel like whatever you do, your decisions are either overlooked or simply forgotten, you lose a sense of moral responsibility that most other people cultivate and mature as they age. Not only that, but this right being lost can have serious long-term effects of a child's life. Not only can they easily turn themselves into a spiteful person capable of great malicious acts, but they can also transform themselves into an individual who is not at all usable as we see it. Although they seem to function properly, they struggle to have much of the inherent knowledge that "average" children do about social groups. Interestingly, when a parent attempts to excessively socialize their child by encouraging them to do basically whatever they want, they not only set them up for disappointment, but at the same time set them on the road to being socially inept, insecure autistic children unable to communicate and connect with people who would normally be their natural peers.

It's strange how all of this goes back to how greedy a parent can be with his kids. Though there are the "true" parents, of course, as we deem them, who would basically do anything to make their child happy while retaining a social hierarchy and a sense of responsibility for them. Although there are many distinct and often contrasting opinions of what constitutes a perfect parent, most people agree that it is better for most children to have a caring and strict family. Such guardians aren't so stern that they might be seen as a traditional parent of "Drill Sergeant," or so loose and doting that they might be called parents of the helicopter, but they usually find their room somewhere in the middle of those two extremes. Those parents are much more likely to be able to make "healthy" and "natural" kids who work just fine and are more than able to thrive within the rest of our society without any other intervening influences. Instead, completely on the other side of that continuum, you have what we find to be "evil" parents, who lack the patience or desire to allow themselves treat their children as individuals rather than objects for their amusement or as trophy cases for their pride. How we find imperfect parents as perfect parents appears in many different forms, from too loose to not lax enough. It should be noted that in such situations this kind of bad parenting creates "bad babies," but— a bit like we think of bad owners, not bad pets— the child's misery almost always lies with the adult, who has neglected their "work" as a parent to keep their child healthy and as comfortable as practicable, despite the environment.

There are many avenues to go wrong, of course, and almost all of them are controllable stuff, though some of them are not. There are certain things we can just never expect to control in our lives. There are things we can actively try to avoid, to swerve on our life's road to avoid crossing paths with some unsightly occurrence, but sometimes it just can't help. Things like that happen, and it's easier to be ready for it than to be willing to give up ship if you hit a bump on the track. In reality, the feeling takes us to the other major factor in negative thinking— not just how we are treated in our homes as children, but the atmosphere in which we communicate with our peers. This is in part in reference to the public education system, although it might also be taken to refer to the much wider scale of today's ever-changing society.

Simply put, the sort of environment that develops in generation after generation as preteens and young adults change and changes as different generations pass across life stages. From the laxer and more carefree world of children in the 80s and 90s, or what is referred to as "Gen X"— which is perhaps the coolest name imaginable for a bunch of 30-somethings— to the more modern social atmosphere that has welcomed children, particularly in the US, with more stressful news than ever before. As the line between fear mongering and simple alert is increasingly blurred, the way children respond and take in details theoretically often changes when their sensitization increases. Although Gen Y, or "millennials," which is the group that is now mostly in their twenties, has been relatively normal with this rapidly changing culture, even psychologists who have conducted studies of young people's mental states agree that the levels of stress, depression, and anxiety are growing year after year, now at the equivalent of an institutionalized patient in the sixties. With that in mind, we now look to the generation that is actually in high school and higher education, Generation Z. Gen Z, as we know it, is undoubtedly the most stressed out, sleep deprived, nervous generation ever, and the one that follows after it is likely to continue the pattern. So; what went wrong in so many lives to make this such a drastic change, such an unprecedented plunge in our last frontier mental state— our student?

The answer comes directly from the public education system as many would expect. With a relatively new drive to be popular, more kids are throwing themselves into a program that gets a little tougher every year, working hard to join extracurricular activities that take up even more of their time just to get into the college they think will help them reach that goal, to be able to live a happy and fulfilling life. Most people have the idea hammered into them that if they work hard enough they're never going to suffer as much in life as those who don't work as hard. This is simply not true, since most students learn very quickly. In reality, the opposite is true— those students who drive themselves are often the ones who end up hurting more when they go on to college, when they are piled up with even more education and are now faced with the burdens of life without parental supervision or the warmth of their loved ones right in front of them. Rather, they have to face the world entirely alone now; at least, that's how it looks and how it feels to many students today.

Once you start feeling trapped, you feel isolated. Some students, especially college students who now have substantially less interaction with their loved ones than they did while living at home, report feeling much more lonely. Negative thinking goes along with that isolation. Feeling isolated from your loved ones and your mates, and experiencing immense pressure to succeed without seeing the true value of pursuing a fulfilling career in life, most graduates, even those who have been the most successful and motivated of their peers earlier in life, will plunge into a frightening spiral of self-doubt and hatred. That can spiral out of control very easily and become a challenge that may not be fully recognized by those students, or know how to fix if they do.

As it happens, this kind of reasoning has been more or less normalized with Gen Z in particular. Whether it's for college or high school students, this way of thinking so little of yourself that it has driven up the tension even more, as an odd circular and inadequate way to cope with that stress spread like wildfire — especially with the help of a still relatively new tool for teens, social media, throughout culture. The social media can be a big boost in spreading the gospel of other students connected to young people who otherwise feel like they have no one to communicate with or reach out to. While social media is most certainly something of a saving grace, it can also be a crutch for many people, particularly those students who are especially susceptible to coercion and manipulation when their other alternative is to be all alone. Yet frankly, not everybody on social media is a good influence or someone whose strategies work for everyone, or anyone else. While that much is clear, it can still be a psychologically and emotionally challenge for students to determine whether to be alone or to feel connected within a society that is, at its heart, toxic to all involved parties.

How can anyone ever expect to get stronger with the kind of mentality that becomes the hidden enemy for many young people being normalized? Actually things aren't as grim as they might seem. In fact, while there are a large number of young people, especially those in Generation Z, who think this way, who are self-deprecating for the sake of using humor as a sort of coping mechanism, there is another, even more recent surge in the actions of young people and teens that takes advantage of the impact well-known social media influencers have on each other and on their viewers. That way of thinking critically and being socially "happy"-offers young people a path and social affirmation to join such social media influencers and reach out and genuinely seek support. If, previously, the notion of suffering in silence for the dark beauty was alluring, and was the only style that those influencers promoted and supported, today those very same public figures are at the forefront of the discussion about how we cope with our pressures, both the older and younger generations in the modern world. Most importantly, tension builds in crowds with social media influencers, and many of them with a purer heart feel the need to fix the friction to resolve the very real mental health crisis we have in classrooms that affect children and teenagers much more easily than in the past generations. Today, the debate is not only conducted on social media by younger people, but is also taken into account by older people, merely because that dangerous situation becomes too noisy, too clear, to be overlooked or pushed aside any longer. The mental health of youth and that youth's negative thinking is so strong and unhealthy now, and we must all come together as a society and as a world to make a concerted effort to help those in great need. Whether they are our babies, the friends of our children or the peers we fear are in danger of succumbing to their own terrible thoughts, we who serve the rest of the world are, in some sense, personally responsible for those who cannot mentally care for themselves for whatever purpose. People, parents, elders, mates, colleagues, and superiors, must step up and care for each other, and protect and support those who don't know how to help themselves — such as the rule of any environment, no matter how cutthroat; everyone within the community needs each other, and they all benefit from each other's abilities and strengthen each other in their shortcomings.

So, as we go forward with that information, I hope it gives you a little insight on what sorts of things young people, and all people around the world, are experiencing within their own minds. Read it so that you can learn how to help those around you, those you love and those you care for, if you're not just doing this to support yourself. For help other victims of something you do not need to be a victim of something. It is the camaraderie that comes with facing the world in all its terrors that brings people together and maintains a relationship in which all sides recognize their obligations and shield each other from other things, or from themselves. Whether it's simply talking to that person or consciously ensuring they get the support they might need, do your part to make sure people around you are taken care of. Denying treatment to others, and the knowledge that they are cherished is also cruelly revoking the person's meaning of life.

CHAPTER 6

HANGING IN THE BALANCE

When, in some way or another, you are simply someone who indulges in theory a lot, you have undoubtedly pondered the true importance of keeping things relatively orderly. As I said in this book before, voicing the balance you want in your life is so incredibly important. Leaning toward an extreme one way or another will eventually only lead to more frustration of feeling unfulfilled. That's also why a lot of people say you might have too much, really. It's not hard to overwhelm anything you like or love, or feel like you need. While this applies to binge-eating, some kind of compulsion, or just the desire to be satisfied by getting too far into something, an obsession or a passion or something completely different, the risk of too much or too little is actually far larger than you think.

Also, we have no idea of the risks of either doing too much or too little of something. Normally, when we notice a bad thing that we normally do and want to stop as soon as we can, we quickly try to stop it all at once, like cutting cold turkey when you used to smoke a cigarette a day. It has not only been in the way that it isn't good for you, it has weakened you and your body physically. It has the ability to send your body and mind into something like a panic state, too disturbed by your conflicting actions to do anything but keep watching with abject horror as you swing back and forth from top to bottom, from left to right, to bottom, from extreme to extreme to extreme, with no real idea of your advancement. We would like to do that because it feels good. When we can tell we left quicker and more profoundly than our colleagues we feel so much more accomplished. Everything can quickly and easily transform into a peer-to-peer rivalry, even stuff that should be to our very own gain. Yet, that's not the way it should be. If you want to stop doing something, make sure you can keep track of your progress— whether that includes tracking stuff you do to get rid of your toxic and destructive thought habits, or joining a group online or in person with someone like you who can help and support you when you need to, it doesn't matter in what medium you consider a support system, but it's always nice. Vocalizing your success and throwing yourself out when you want to leave something, is also really good. It not only eliminates the temptation to separate yourself from anyone you care about, but it also persuades you to follow up on the promises you may have made to the camera and posted online in a blur of the moment, fire of passion. That way, take your competitive spirit and use it to your benefit. Challenge yourself regularly, to make sure you don't take any prisoners. Having a consistent and aggressive attitude about kicking the habit is one of the many keys of effectively breaking a bad habit, other than juggling and knowing you have a good support system. The more you are able to detach the hatred you have for yourself, and pin it on that bad habit instead, the happier you'll be in the long run.

Of course, the risks that may happen when you don't take the advice and choose to swing back and forth from one extreme side of something to another must be taken into consideration. Take water, for example,— a need to be alive, an absolute necessity if you want to be safe or usable. Water is incredibly healthy, it has no calories, it refreshes you, it can help with weight loss and it has many other small yet proven benefits to wellness. Therefore, somebody who is trying to get more hydrated will plunge head-first into their latest obsession on drinking more water. While this does not cause a lot of problems in and of itself, it can evolve to be something that causes considerable damage to your life.

For course everyone knows the risks of not getting enough water to drink. Your mouth begins to feel gritty when you're dehydrated, so you start feeling sick. You lose the sharp focus that you might have had when you were hydrated, and you become far less efficient all around you than you would be if you were properly hydrated earlier that day. When that hydration occurs, the distinction between what is actually exhausted and what entails being rushed to the hospital and getting to have an IV in your arm can be hard to draw. If you become very dehydrated, your condition can deteriorate rapidly and very quickly, even without you knowing. This is what happens to most people who are suffering from a sunstroke— they simply don't know when to find, then they are now approaching the point where they have to drink water if they don't want to unexpectedly become weak. Because they don't actually know how to identify these signals, many of those who suffer from sunstroke are victims of that sort of thing and are blamed for it. We live with the knowledge that we risk their safety and perhaps even their life by stubbornly following someone's advice.

On the flip side of that, a lot of people compulsively drink water. This may be trying to get rid of their oral fixation, sometimes even quitting smoking, or it may just be because that person happens to be on a new fixation with some form of technique of wellness or weight loss. While water is a good way to lose weight and decrease appetite, people who drink tons of it often don't get the rewarding benefits they may want. As I said, the results are gradual and rather mild, if not balanced by that person's workout and a shift in eating habits. At any point, a lot of people only enjoy drinking water for their mental and physical pleasure. Although in its own practice, just for its own sake, that's good, some people go too far with that. Obsessive people who may be hell-bound to their current obsession may over-hydrate, which is as dangerous as being dangerously dehydrated. When you drink an excessive amount of water in a relatively short time frame, a time frame comparable to the amount of water you ingest, the sodium level in your blood will plummet and can have extremely harmful and even lethal consequences on your system. The main cause of death from drinking too much water is just that, the disease of having incredibly low sodium in your blood, often called "water poisoning." Though it may sound a bit crazy, water poisoning takes a significant number of lives each year. There's also a trend for younger people to drink more water right now, as the dark look of being depraved has fallen from favor and the modern image of good skin and good health has come in instead to replace the aesthetic. This drive could easily sway other young people to put themselves at greater risk for this kind of disease which can be extremely dangerous for them and their safety. And, though you should definitely drink plenty of water every day, of course, there's something to say about doing anything to the full, no matter what it is.

Still, what about things that aren't real, may you ask? Yeah, you may have too much or too little food, too much or too little water, too little or too much sleep, exercise, sex, what do you have. Yet, is there really something to tell about the possibility of overloading? Too much confidence? Feeling too happy?

The reaction to that is, put it simply, absolutely. When we gage what is and what is not too much or too little of something so elusive and intangible as love, confidence, hope, happiness or sorrow, we may say from personal experience within ourselves and with others that, yes, you may have too much or too little of something spiritual.

Also, the scale of events that don't have a physical manifestation of a physical basis is much harder to judge; certain people can actually suffer from depression. In reality, the disorder is heart strings that break down from pressure to heart, allowing the heart itself to crumble in on itself and kill the body from within. While it is a physical reaction to something more abstract, it may be due to intense emotion, namely desperation, the strain to the heart. Typically that would be something like a heartbreak— no pun intended— including breakup from a longtime partner, a loved one's death, or something else just as crippling the human. This sorrow can destroy a person solely in the emotional sense, but it can actually destroy them from that sort of misery in the literal sense of fatality. Likewise, given the context and the correct degree, rage can also have this sort of effect on someone. Any feeling, actually, can have an effect on somebody like this. It's just something that poses a far more real danger to us as humans than we might have known before. Emotions and passion will flame us out, in much calmer terms. For example, those things definitely aren't anything that causes death or equally extreme effects, but they're nothing to ignore the findings. Remember that, the first few months are perfect when dating someone new. You feel so deeply in love, like this guy has to be the perfect match for you, your always and forever. You feel stronger than you have ever been, and you burst to shout out to the universe how much you love them, and they feel exactly the same way. We want to show you all off and you two are joined at the hip. Yet, unexpectedly, and from nowhere, the "spark" just seems to die suddenly. Immediately the two of you are no longer as connected, it feels overwhelming to be around them, you no longer go on spontaneous walks late at night, no more of those fun and friendly nights, and what you used to view as their adorable quirks and eccentricity are now things you can't bear, things that get in the way of your already busy and stressful life. You feel awful, and so they and neither of you have any idea why. You don't think something bad happened to tear you apart from one another in your relationship, but you don't know how to explain this abrupt "death" of what you might have thought was your passion. And, what the fuck did you two do?

The harsh reality is, you weren't even in love from the beginning— you were completely infatuated with your partner nonetheless. Most people would tell you that you fell out of love, but more of the reverse is actually true. To fact, you're beginning the first stage of actually loving someone, which allows you to step out of a relationship's first phase, also called the "Honeymoon Phase." This process has a lot of dopamine and other reward chemicals swirling around within the brain for pretty much all the time, and it's just those hormones, serotonin and adrenaline and all the rest that make you feel so enthusiastic towards them. You are still not having a genuine connection. And you feel incredibly in love with your ideal self and yourself. When you sound so excited about yourself and your partner's interpretations alike, the subconscious just interprets the emotion as "true love," rather than what it truly is under the rose-colored glasses — infatuation that eventually dies after a few months. The honeymoon period of a relationship lasts from a few months to a year and a half, and after that, you know the sensation of an inevitable drop-off. You no longer feel like you miss them because you don't have a constant stream of hormones running into you anymore. But, now you have the ruts from those chemicals in your head. You have room in your head where those thoughts and hormones will flow through you like they usually do, but their intrusion during the honeymoon phase has made the part of your brain that is interacting with your significant other fried. The brain needs time to recover again and you will feel as though the "spark" between the two of you has totally died up until then. This part of love almost never lasts as long as the other phase which came a few months ago. It depends on the person and the strength of their honeymoon phase and their significant other. Most partners do not make it past that point but those who do are rewarded with a relationship that is often endgame or at least rather long-term and ideally satisfying. After the dead flame period, the "heart" reignites in the form of the next step, and the cycle begins again, revived now that the infatuation has been replaced by a more genuine, stronger, truer passion in the third and final phase of most endgame relationships— the phase in which you really know more about each other, become best friends on top of your relationship, and become unified for good this time.

While that's a tangent, it shows you can potentially have too much love as long as that love comes in chemicals type. If we do them too much we get sick of things that we do. That's why, even though it's a great song, it gets killed when a decent song gets heard way too much on the radio. We dislike it, because how much we hear it against our will is becoming irritating.

Too much, too little of something, too big or too small, the way we teach our kids, the way we grow our kids, the way we live as babies. All these things converge and work to make the current phenomenon of negative thinking what we believe to be. The way to stop is in the hands of the people who made it, and the families that are hurting because of it. It's good if you want to give up on your negative thinking and become happier and healthier. Yet, I don't think you'd want to do that if you'd read this far into a book about breaking just that bad habit. Just remember that, no matter what, you have the ability to do whatever you think is right inside of you. The power is in you, it's always been within you and it'll always be within you. All matters is whether you have any confidence in yourself and the people who love you and value you, or not. Those are the ones you need most, except that you are yourself.

CHAPTER 7

WHAT IT MEANS TO BE POSITIVE

You encountered people who are insufferably happy in your life. Everything just falls off their back and into the puddles that they play in like a kid. We seem so curiously positive and happy-go-lucky; it is almost as though they have never received bad news in their entire lives. Not only is watching them going through life like every day is indescribably bright kind of off-putting, but it could also make you very worried about their mental health. After all, you've probably learned more than just that, under a grin, is often a very lonely, very broken, and very frightened guy. It can be difficult to keep the façade intact but some people manage to do it well and do it for a very long time before the cracks begin to show up. You might say to yourself, maybe this is one of those men. Within their metaphorical armor, they never reveal the chink; they still support but never ask for it in exchange. I could go on and on with this hypothetical person for ever, because they're all known. Yet, you would be right — none really is that optimistic. If they are, it may potentially be as dangerous as having negative thoughts in the normal sense.

Simply put, what I mean by that is you've got to have a balance in all aspects of your life. I've scratched all kinds of people for being just a little too pessimistic, not giving in to all of them, victimizing themselves, and doing numerous other things that feel better at the moment but don't really fix something, but maybe all of those things don't even scratch the surface of what some people do is worse than worrying about themselves and others. As I said in the last essay, going from one extreme to the next just causes mental shock; it throws you into a panic state and leaves you confused about what to do with yourself. To act excessively is something like a purely human trait, in a strange way. It's weird, it's dangerous, and it inevitably ends in disaster, but it's a tendency that we can't all seem to be kicked in.

When you go through your life constantly or almost constantly pushing yourself to be positive and happy, you are focused on killing the reasonable part of yourself which is especially good at pointing out faults and weaknesses in situations. The key of a compromise between being a scathing pessimist and getting the unhealthy feelings that have been brought under the microscope this whole time, and being a scathing optimist— someone who is so hopeful that it's unhealthy and, in many instances, delusional — is being able to step back to examine the flaws in something but remain happy while making adjustments.

Although it seems similarly dangerous, any time you try to detach yourself from your shortcomings, just as long as you take a serious, long look at them in a practical, yet vital way. It harms not only our ego, but it affects our performance as well, as we bind ourselves to feedback and take it as a personal insult. If we feel like one person in our lives hates us— even if they don't really— then that same distrust is about everybody else in our lives, and we flee into the safe space in our own minds, where we can disappear underneath all that negative thinking and victimization until someone is willing to show that they matter enough for us to pull us out of our mental canyon. However, as we consciously decide not to take things personally, the unintentionally hurtful comment will turn into something much better, something more positive than you can use to strengthen yourself rather than having the remark to get you down and add fuel to your negative thinking. Nonetheless, we always like to believe that somehow, one day, we're going to have someone there to save us from just about everything in the world, our knight in shining armor or just a friend or mother to hug us and support us and make us feel like we don't have to do anything, as it's not our fault.

Unfortunately, the truth isn't almost that pretty— you need to be the one and only one to dig yourself out of your emotional canyon. While it may be frightening to do so, we will be our own knight in shining armor. Collectively we have to abandon the idea that someone will come to save you whenever we want, whenever we need them. This sort of thinking is what makes us compliant, submissive, and what helps to keep us in that cage of negative thoughts, which lets us sink ever further into our brains. We're slipping further and further into the trap of not having to take the lead and go forward with our own lives. That's something far closer to the truth sadly.

While nobody ever wants to do something on their own, people who have that kind of negative thinking do it very rarely because they want to. Most don't want to talk like that, but in a way they know it's just like their "programming." Their entire lives, or at least most of their childhood, has been packed with their parents or guardians protecting them and assuring them that whatever mess they do, it is not their fault and it is not their job to clean up for it. No, at the time the burden fell entirely upon them, the parent or guardian who watched over the boy. In fact, caring for oneself is not the child's work, simply because no one else will. We have no idea how to take responsibility for their actions, and they don't know how to take responsibility for doing something wrong in the first place without having people turn against them. However, here's another secret— what you do doesn't initially identify you as a human. The opportunities that you get, the luck you have, don't really rely on you. What is reflective of you, however, is how you react to the cards you have been dealt over the course of your life. If you choose to disregard the weight of what you've done, it shows strongly that you're somebody who hates accountability, somebody who possibly can't handle commitment, and many other things that aren't exactly great to have said about you. Yet, no matter what you've done wrong in the past if you courageously own it, it represents the exact opposite of you. Even though you have done something wrong, sometimes something is simply inexcusable for the task or the work or whatever circumstance it may have happened in, it reflects well on you that you accepted it and at least put forth an honest effort of goodness to better yourself and the condition in which you were positioned. That not only needs the confidence within you to take responsibility, but it also requires a lot of positive — or at least realistic — thinking. As we leave high school as kids to go to whatever college we may have chosen, we always abandon a life built for us all our lives. Whether or not we admit it, whether we like it or not, we really start missing the order. This came from our parents, yes, and back then our least favorite teachers, but it was still order, something that gave us a sense of purpose, and that at the time meant a lot to us. We just loved not knowing exactly what to do. Even getting to follow the instructions throughout the day is soothing. When we leave high school and go off to live alone, we always leave behind our parents and teachers and we have to start building our own foundation. That, can be mortifying in itself. Even though we may be very individualized and autonomous, we as humans naturally pack animals and never like having to be surrounded by people we consider foreign. They just don't work like other animals, flying alone, living alone and working alone in the best way. Even though in today's modern world, learning to live like that could potentially turn out to be better for our mental wellbeing.

The point is all of the negative thoughts aren't toxic. The universe is messy sometimes and bad things happen, it is an important part of the way we all live. It's happened before and it's bound to happen to you and everyone else. You don't have success every day but don't let that either stop you from trying to find the evil in it. In everything that we are there are good things and good people, in everything we do. The planet is working like this. You can be sad— you can have bad days and you will be guided through by the people who love you. You can have those feelings of rage and deep sorrow. You can weep and yell or leap for happiness, but realize that without the other, you can't have one, so know how to have both in your life. If you can learn how to put the balance into practice, you'll have a more fulfilled life, both good and bad.

HOW TO IMPROVE YOUR EMOTIONAL INTELLIGENCE

1. Utilize an assertive style of communicating.

Assertive contact is going a long way in earning respect without being too hostile or defensive. Individuals who are emotionally intelligent know how to communicate their thoughts and desires openly while respecting others.

2. Respond instead of reacting to conflict.

Emotional outbursts and feelings of anger are normal during contrasting instances. The person with an emotional intelligence knows how to remain calm in stressful situations. We do not make impulsive decisions which can lead to even greater problems. We recognize that the aim is a settlement in times of conflict, and we make a conscious decision to concentrate on how their actions and words agree with that.

3. Utilize active listening skills.

Throughout discussions, people with emotional intelligence listen for clarification, rather than just waiting for their turn to speak. Until responding, they ensure they understand what's being said. We even take care of the nonverbal aspects of a discussion. It avoids misunderstandings, allows the listener to respond appropriately and displays respect for the person to whom they talk.

4. Be motivated.

Emotionally intelligent people are self-motivated, and others are inspired by their mindset. We are setting goals and they are resilient to challenges.

5. Practice ways to maintain a positive attitude.

Don't underestimate your attitude's might. A negative attitude will quickly corrupt others if one person permits it. Emotionally smart people have an understanding of the moods of those around them and their behavior is controlled appropriately. We learn what to do to get a good day and a positive outlook. This might involve having a great breakfast or lunch, investing in Morning Prayer or meditation, or keeping meaningful quotations at their office or screen.

6. Practice self-awareness.

People with emotional intelligence are self-conscious and intuitive. They become mindful of their own feelings, and how those around them can be influenced. We also focus on the thoughts and body language of others, and use that information to improve their communication skills.

7. Take critique well.

A significant part of improving your emotional intelligence is being able to take criticism. Instead of becoming upset or angry, people with high EQ take a few minutes to consider where the criticism comes from, how it impacts someone or their own success and how they can resolve any issues constructively.

8. Empathize with others.

Those who are mentally wise learn how to empathize. We recognize that empathy is a quality that shows strength in the heart, not vulnerability. Empathy allows people, on a basic human level, to respond to others. It opens the door to mutual respect and understanding among people with different opinions and different situations.

9. Utilize leadership skills.

Emotionally smart people possess excellent leadership skills. We have high standards, which set an example for others to follow. You have great decision-making and problem-solving capabilities and take initiative. It makes a higher and more efficient level of performance both at work and in life.

10.   Be approachable and sociable.

Those who are socially savvy come off as approachable. They are laughing and showing off a good look. We use appropriate social skills based on their relationship to whoever we are around. We have excellent interpersonal skills, and we know how to communicate plainly, through vocal or nonverbal contact.

To those who understand basic human psychology, many of these abilities may seem best suited. Although high EQ skills can come to inherently empathic people more quickly, they can be learned by anyone. More empathetic people just need to practice becoming more self-conscious and aware of how they communicate with others. By using those measures, you will be well on the way to through your level of emotional intelligence.

HOW TO BOOST SELF CONFIDENCE

1. Stay away from negativity and bring on the positivity

This is the time to evaluate your inner circle in real terms, like friends and family. This is a difficult one, but it's time to consider seriously walking away from those people who put you down and shred your trust.

Be confident, even if you don't see it as yet. Bring some constructive energy into your relationships with others, and hit the running track, ready to launch your next job. Stop focusing on your life's problems, and start focusing on ideas and making positive improvements instead.

2. Change your body language and image

It is here where stance, smile, eye contact and voice come into play slowly. Just the simple act of pulling back your shoulders gives the impression to others that you're a confident person. Not only will laughing make you feel better but it will make others feel more relaxed around you. Imagine a person with a good posture and a smile and you'll imagine someone who's confident in himself.

Look at the person you're referring to, not your shoes— keeping the eye contact indicates confidence. Next, speak slowly. Evidence has shown that those who take the time to speak slowly and clearly feel more faith in themselves and look more positive towards others. The added bonus is that they really will be able to understand what you're doing.

Go the extra mile to style your hair, put on a clean shave, and dress up beautifully. This not only makes you feel better for yourself, but also makes others more likely to view you as positive and self-confident. A great tip: If you buy a new dress, first try wearing it at home to get over any malfunctions in your closet before going out.

3. Don't accept failure and get rid of the negative voices in your head

Never concede. Always embrace default. Everything has a remedy, so why would you want to throw in the towel? Build your new mantra to this. Success through considerable difficulty is a big catalyst for morale.

Low self-confidence is often induced by the constant trail of negative thoughts going through our heads. If you're constantly bashing yourself and thinking that you're not nice enough, aren't pretty enough, aren't clever enough or talented enough, and you're building a prophecy that is self-fulfilling. Within your brain you are what you are teaching, and that's not healthy. The next time you hear the negative in your mind, turn it to a positive affirmation right away and hold it up until it reaches the level of a lift of self-confidence.

4. Be prepared

Know all you need to learn about your industry, career, presentation — whatever's next on the "to win" list. If you're confident and have the skills to help it, your self-confidence will grow.

5. For tough times, when all else fails: Create a great list

Life is full of obstacles and there are times when our self-confidence is hard to keep up. Sit down now and make a list of all the things you're grateful for in your career, and another list of all the accomplishments you're proud to do. When your lists are full, paste them on your fridge door, on your office wall, on your bathroom mirror— somewhere you can easily remember what an amazing life you've had and what a wonderful person you really are. When you find that your self-confidence is dwindling, take a look at those lists and let yourself be encouraged by you all over again.

HOW TO IMPROVE YOUR SELF-ESTEEM

1. Use positive affirmations correctly

Positive statements like "I'll be a great success!" They are extremely popular, but they have one critical problem— they tend to make people with a low self-esteem feel worse. Why? Because when we are weak in self-esteem, these claims are actually too contradictory to our existing beliefs. Interestingly, for one subset of people, optimistic affirmations work— those whose self-esteem is already high. Tweak them to make them more convincing for affirmations that work when your self-esteem is lagging behind. For example, "I'm going to be a huge hit, for starters! "I will persevere before I excel!"

2. Identify your competencies and develop them

Self-esteem is created by showing real potential and success in areas of our lives that matter to us. If you're proud to be a good cook so throw more dinner parties. If you're a good runner, log in and qualify for the runs. In brief, define your core competencies and find opportunities and jobs that prioritize them.

3. Learn to accept compliments

One of the trickiest facets of raising self-esteem is that we seem to be more prone to praise when we feel bad about ourselves— even though that is when we need them the most. And set yourself the objective of tolerating comments when you collect them even if they make you (and they'll) awkward. The best way to avoid the reflexive responses of batting away comments is to plan simple set replies and teach yourself to use them immediately whenever you get good feedback (e.g., "Thank you" or "How kind of you to say"). The tendency to reject or rebuff compliments will fade in time— which will also be a good sign that your self-esteem will grow stronger.

4. Eliminate self-criticism and introduce self-compassion

Unfortunately, by being self-critical, we are likely to damage it even more when our self-esteem is weak. Because our aim is to improve our self-esteem, self-criticism (which is almost always completely useless, even if it sounds compelling) needs to be replaced by self-compassion. Actually, as the self-critical inner monolog kicks in, ask yourself what you would say to a dear friend if they were in your position (we seem to be far more forgiving towards friends than we are towards ourselves) and apply those remarks to yourself. Doing so will discourage critical thoughts from undermining your self-esteem, and instead help build it up.

5. Affirm your real worth

The following technique has been shown to help revive your self-esteem after it has suffered a blow: Make a list of attributes that are important in the particular context. For starters, if you have been declined by your partner, list attributes that make you a good relationship candidate (e.g. being trustworthy or emotionally available); if you have struggled to get a job promotion, list qualities that make you a desirable employee (you have a strong work ethic or are responsible). Then choose one of the items on your list and write a short article (one or two paragraphs) on why other people are important and likely to enjoy the content in the future. Do the workout for a week every day, or whenever you need a lift of self-esteem.

The bottom line is enhancing self-esteem requires a bit of effort as it entails cultivating and sustaining healthy mental behaviors but doing so, and doing so properly, would deliver a great emotional and psychological return on your investment.

HOW TO IMPROVE YOUR DECISION MAKING

1. Cost-Benefit Analysis

Without reaching the final decision, it's necessary to weigh the pros and cons and make sure you make the best possible choice. It includes a cost-benefit analysis in which you analyze the result on any (positive and negative) path. This will help you see the cost of success, or the stuff you overlook when you choose one choice over another.

2. Narrow Your Options

For simplify the study of costs-benefits, restrict yourself for fewer options. When we are faced with more options, the greater the complexity of making a final decision. Further options will lead to more disappointment as we find all the missing opportunities and wonder if we could have selected one of the many other possible paths. Narrowing the options as such will result in better peace of mind.

3. Evaluate the Significance

How long would you wait mulling over a possible decision? Ten seconds to this? Ten minutes, right? 10 Days or more? It all depends on what is at stake. Determine the importance of a decision (How much of an impact will it have on my life? How much will it cost me?) to eliminate agonizing indecision, then set a deadline accordingly.

4. Don't Sweat the Small Stuff

If it is something as easy as choosing where to go for lunch or what to watch on tv, try to keep things in perspective and keep the decision-making time frame to a minimum. This is closely tied to determining the meaning of a decision— if it doesn't significantly affect you or others, then don't waste time arguing constantly about your choices.

5. Do Your Research

This may seem intuitive but when it comes to making major decisions — new cell phone or tablet, car brand, etc. — taking in the time and effort to thoroughly educate yourself about your future investment will mean the difference between product fulfillment and constant dissatisfaction.

6. Get a Well-Informed Opinion

It's more than just studying a decision's facts and details — having a personal opinion can also boost your decision making by giving you the confidence and reassurance that you're making the right choice. Whether it's telling your auto mechanic buddy before buying a car or reviewing Consumer Reports before buying a new kitchen appliance, informed opinions are really beneficial.

HOW TO EXERCISE YOUR BRAIN

1. Use all your senses

A research conducted in 2015 suggests using all the senses could help strengthen the brain.

Consider doing exercises that involve all five of your senses at the same time to give your senses and your brain a workout. You can try to bake a batch of cookies, visit a farmer's market, or try a new restaurant while you're focusing on smelling, touching, degusting, seeing and hearing all at once.

2. Learn a new skill

Not only is learning a new talent fun and interesting, it can also help reinforce the links within the brain.

Research from 2014 also suggests that learning a new ability in older adults will help to improve memory function.

You've always wanted to learn how to do something there? Maybe you want to learn how to fix your vehicle, use some software program or ride a horse? Now you've got another good reason to learn the new skill.

3. Teach a new skill to someone else

One of the best ways to extend your learning is to teach another person a talent.

You need to practice it after you have learned a new skill. This needs you to explain the concept to someone else, and correct any mistakes you make. Learn to swing a golf club for example and then show a friend the moves.

4. Listen to or play music

Want an easy way to boost your imaginative brain power? The solution may be to turn a music on.

Listening to positive melodies allows to create more innovative solutions, relative to being in silence, according to a 2017 report. That suggests, cranking up some feel-good music will help boost your creativity and creative thinking.

And if you want to learn how to play music, now is a great time to start, because at any point in your life, your brain is able to learn new things. That's why you're never too old to start playing a keyboard, guitar or even percussion instrument.

5. Take a new route

When it comes to your everyday tasks don't get stuck in a rut. Instead, be prepared to try out new ways of doing the same things.

Choose a different route to get to work every week or try another mode of transportation, such as walking or using public transportation instead of driving. A simple change will help your brain and you might be surprised at how easy it is to change your thinking.

6. Meditate

Meditation on a daily basis will relax the body, ease your breathing and reduce stress and anxiety.

But did you know it can also help to fine-tune your memory and improve the ability of your brain to process information?

Find a quiet spot, close your eyes and meditate for five minutes each day.

7. Learn a new language

A 2012 literature study showed unanimously the many cognitive advantages of being able to speak more than one language.

Bilingualism can lead to better memory, enhanced visual-spatial skills and higher levels of creativity, according to numerous studies. Also being fluent in more than one language will help you transition between different tasks more quickly, and delay the onset of mental decline due to ageing.

The good news is that reaping the benefits of learning a new language is never too late. According to experts, you can enhance your memory by becoming a student of a new language at any time in your life, and develop certain mental functions.

8. Take up tai chi

It's no secret that in many respects tai chi will help your fitness including your mental health. Plus, when life seems out of control, it can help stabilize you too.

Taking regular Tai Chi practice can help to reduce stress, improve the quality of sleep and improve memory. A research in 2013 showed that the long-term practice of tai chi could cause structural changes in the brain, leading to an increase in brain volume.

Beginners do their part by taking a class to master the various moves. But when you learn the fundamentals, you can practice tai chi anywhere, anywhere.

9. Focus on another person

If you communicate with someone every time you take care of four things about them. You may note their shirt or pants color. Were they wearing spectacles? Have they got a hat on and if so, what kind of cap? What is their hair color?

If you plan to recall four things, make a mental note and then return to it later in the day. Write down what about those four specifics you recall.

HOW TO STOP NEGATIVE THINKING

1. Speak To The Negative Thought

Practice being aware of those feelings as they come up. Should you feel tired, thirsty, frustrated, depressed or anything else? We don't go anywhere as we try to ignore negative thoughts, we keep popping again. Recognize these to combat them. Let your inner voice say, "I hear a negative thought; it's a story that I'm telling myself and it's not real."

2. Get Around Positive People

Want to catch some cold? Get around with a cough, people. I'm not sure the suggestion really stands, but it does mean much to me when I mentor someone. I see many people associating with like-minded and often negative people as they try to change something, like a career, in their lives. Negatives aren't constructive. Physically get around positivity, through your ears and your pupils.

3. Don't Expect Everything To Be Perfect

It can be frustrating to expect everything to be flawless and it robs you of true happiness. Make sure that your dream of success really is steeped. Of eg, if you are elevated next year— as planned instead of this year— does one year really mean anything over the long term?

Striving for goals trying to be flawless with a distance to the end state can be a refreshing way to live on your own terms.

4. Work With An Active Mindset

A bulletproof mentality is no alternative. It's important to discover a method that appeals for you. The group works better when teaching different types of clientele (executives, millennials and entrepreneurs). The one thing I found to be true and realistic is that no standard practice exists. Your attitude process is entirely tailored and will change based on what restricting values you are trying to remove, and what positive traits you are trying to instill in your daily routine. "Stick with it" is the most valuable advice I can give. Get into a routine, figure out what fits and don't hesitate until you've perfected the system you're using.

5. Develop A Positive Morning Routine

Early in the morning, thoughts begin. If the thought is controlled by a tyrant, they rule their life. Negative thinking will slow down a leader. Leaders have to captivate every thought by combining thoughts of terror with thoughts of hope and faith. One method that great thinkers use is to build a morning routine where they read something positive and encouraging every morning.

6. Just Breathe

You need to slow down everything to avoid negative thoughts, and first try to just note them. It will get you more comfort and self-awareness by integrating timers, alerts and actual time blocks into your life to just breathe. Then just breathe them out as you start noticing how many negative thoughts you're having. The key is not comparing yourself or getting caught up in the negative thoughts. Over time, you'll get better at this workout, just like anything else.

7. Become Intentional About Your Attitude

Having a positive attitude is a deliberate action starting as soon as you wake up in the morning. Be conscious as you concentrate on the negative, and make the decision to reflect instead on the positive. Your mindset reflects a decision. You draw what you're focused on so let go of something that doesn't match your interests. The more positive mind-shifts you do, the simpler that becomes.

8. Try The Displacement Theory

Have tried not thinking? Do it, and see what happens sometime. If you want to smash the habits of negative thinking, you have to replace them with something else. At the same moment, no-one can dream of two things. Now, pick something you'd love to do and start working on it; let your ideal project displace the old thoughts.

9. Focus On The Promise, Not The Problem

No matter what your abilities or current work environment are, if you let them live, there will always be grounds for negative thoughts. If you start feeling pessimistic, simply remember why you're there. Reflect on where you are going and why that matters to you. It's about the end goal though, not the difficult parts of the process.

10.   Tap Into The Root Problem

Often negative thinking arises from a problem not seen clearly on the table. I call it the "source question." Sometimes these destructive habits of thought are rooted in us from an early age and have become part of our culture. To transcend these destructive patterns of thought, you have to recognize the deeper-seeded explanation why these trends continue to show up. Then and only then can you tackle the problem.

11. Make A Conscious Choice

Unless you can expose what they are you can't get rid of negative thought patterns. Get to know the negative thoughts and how they get activated. Only with that self-awareness can you begin to identify when it occurs, and make a choice in the moment to change your focus.

WHAT IS EMPATHY HEALING?

Empathy heals. How? Have you ever been so tired, you could hardly get out of bed, but then someone got it right? I helped. It was your mate who brought broth. Her husband was making tea. Your mother called. They gave you drugs not. You have not even met you personally, but their compassion and empathy made you realize that you are not alone.

It can be a long and tough journey when you are recovering from something more than a cough. For the faint-hearted, detoxification is not. Mega successes (a month free of migraines!) can be interspersed with soothing emergencies (the worst of all earache). It is difficult to move about through fear and uncertainty. You can't eat what you used to want or maybe even do stuff that you used to love. Sitting alone with those defeats seems more like being robbed than advancing. It's easier to keep your eyes on the road ahead, with a traveling companion. Faith and hope can be harder to have. Partners don't just let partners withdraw by themselves. Neither parents nor kids do.

Healing a world bereft of empathy

Consider someone who doesn't feel safe in his or her body? Have you ever pondered this? Did you ever wonder how many people feel profoundly vulnerable inside the world?

They are a society devoid of empathy, and it is where society feels most about its lack of children; because the dysfunctional universe is as it is due to adults not fulfilling their emotional needs when they are young. They knew no idea what their emotions were and thus tried to hide them. The effect is a society full of people working under immense deprivation and suffering, which then negatively impacts the world when it is acting out. We maintain a dangerous world from a disembodied mind — from a state of inability to experience the pain, and thus occupy their body.

The intelligence is stronger because of the need for the victim to disassociate themselves from suffering into the mind of thought. Mentation is the location where hurtful, distorted bodies seek relief. Have you ever asked why reason favors Western civilization above emotions to the extent it does? This doesn't help the issue of persistent disembodiment from children to adults, of course. It's a vacillating circle. Ungrounded minds build and perpetuate Western dominant culture. It is run by strong, disembodied intellects, who are deeply afraid to feel. Which, as we can see, is highly dangerous.

The way to get out of the confusion is through. We're not fixing the universe by altering what's "out there;" instead, we're curing it by gradually leaning into what our minds have long resisted.

The world desperately needs people who live out a profound sense of security. A sense of comfort internally fosters a drive to build stability for others and our world. A balanced biology makes safer, life-giving decisions because the thinking-mind is in sync with the body-feel. We do not work independently but as a cohesive network, perceiving life as a single whole.

Healing is the transition from one part to the next. We initiate this process by re-inhabiting the pieces of ourselves that we have long suppressed— the emotions.

The earth heals as we heal, as we give the tired, uncomfortable feelings in our bodies long-awaited empathy; as we approach the delicate human body of our and others as we would a young child — with concern, with a sensitive ear, with a need to be with and sooth.

CONCLUSION

You have come so far to read all of this. It's a surprise how driven you have to be so committed to fixing your outlook and making yourself a happier person. First and foremost I hope you will be able to bring yourself to be congratulated. Beat yourself on the head, sit back and be proud, but you see fit— the most important thing about breaking a pattern of negative thinking is that it doesn't apply to those who only ask others for assistance without doing much about themselves. The only way you can live a better and more meaningful existence is if you can put out your hand and do it yourself. You have to be the one to take the perfect first step towards recovery and strengthening and that's just what you're doing. That's a really admirable thing to do, so I'm sincerely confident you can be proud of making a move forward.

That's another very widespread form of slowly chipping away from your self-deprecation habits — thinking of good things, even the smallest of things. No matter how small you might think it is, no matter how meaningless you might think something you have done is, I would like to congratulate you and do it well. We take this sort of thing so often absolutely for granted, actually. Some activities we do during our morning or evening rituals are so often disregarded. When we get so wrapped up on the things we do wrong, we sometimes find it hard to remember and document the stuff that we do well every single day. When that happens, just take a step back for a moment. Curiously, temporary isolation can be a good idea, though with few and far between times of that detachment, if your negative thinking is particularly unhealthy or dangerous. Take a step back and simply understand that the things you are doing well far outweigh the things you are doing wrong. You'll know even those things that you're still doing incorrectly. That is another thing about us that's crazy — we're learning things. Yet, more often than not, we are really learning things, very quickly. It's a strange thing, but when we start something new we get so caught up in what we can't do yet that we somehow lose the ability to tell what we can do now. Many people say this way of sorting out what we can and can't do, and dwelling on the category "can't," is heavily related to our growth. If you were an animal focused solely on life, you should concentrate on what you have yet to discover, rather than what you already learned. But-in this situation you are not in a position to dwell on that sort of thing. In fact, sometimes we learned how to reflect on our shortcomings and the stuff we haven't accomplished just yet in a positive way that helps us to learn more easily. Then, we began learning how to look at our shortcomings and those mysterious talents not with constructive criticism, but rather with a negative hand. Today, some of us can't help but look at a list of things we really can't do and we feel like we're sad. Because of what kind of world you grew up in, if you are reading this book and connected to at least some of the stuff you've done, you're definitely someone who, as a teenager, had a lot of pressure on you. This burden is hurting and I'm sorry. The burden of trying to surprise your friends or peers with your good grades too badly, feeling upset with yourself when you don't live up to their expectations, the pain you get in bed late that night, worrying about all the things you might easily have done just a little better. If you'd just been working a bit harder; a bit more often if you'd just paid a little more interest in the class the day before. It's awful to feel like you have failed the people you care for, and want to be the most proud of you. Live with the remorse of what you know is making those men, those role models, unhappy in you, is something I would never want for anyone because I do honestly recognize the emotion, I like to think. If you're reading this, you may never have conquered the shame about letting down your parents and teachers, so you've continued to try. You kept trying and you were busy for years and years trying to satisfy them. Maybe as you grew older their standards increased, and with them you were forced to grow faster and faster. You may have lost a little bit of your youth to that addiction and now you like that obsession a little bit of your adult. It hurts feeling like you are doomed to fail them no matter what you do. I understand the pain.

Please know that, no matter what happens today, people will always be proud of you. You should be proud of yourself, above all. For so long, you've come so far and done so much for yourself, suffering and fighting tooth and nail just to keep up with peers. That's why, on the one hand, you have done what you have. The fascination has made you grow up to be competent and acclimatized to stressful environments in a macabre way. On the other hand, doing just that and tempering your competitive spirit has not only exercised your intellect and helped you to deal with stress, anxiety and other people's expectations, but has done the opposite in the process as well. While it made you become more competitive, it pulled you down until you didn't have to be competitive any more. When there were no more expectations for you to follow in school or at home, you were left with that obsessive nature that guided you to always do well and to ignore everything that you had already achieved. Yet, you had to make tough expectations of your own. It was tough but I think you will take a step back to realize how far you have come on your path. You have, after all, come so amazingly fast. See you. Love yourself.

CPSIA information can be obtained
at www.ICGtesting.com
Printed in the USA
BVHW061007040321
601713BV00012B/997